In the Garden with God

Dene Ward

In the Garden with God

P.O. Box 6259, Chillicothe, Ohio 45601
800.300.9778
www.deward.com

Cover design by Jonathan Hardin.

Printed in the United States of America.

ISBN: 978-1-936341-58-0

For my husband, Keith—

The hardest working gardener I know, who has taught his family the value of hard work and the pleasure of sharing with others.

It is the hard-working farmer who ought to have the first share of the crops. (2 Tim 2.6)

Preface

God's people lived in an agricultural society. He always used those references to teach His lessons, and His Son continued that in His time here on the earth. Sowing and reaping, working in vineyards, weeding the field, and cursing an unfruitful fig tree have taught lessons easy for all to understand.

I worry sometimes that our culture will lose that. Not everyone has even a yard with flower beds any more. Maybe urban farmers' markets will fill the bill since we all have to eat, but there is still something lost in translation if you have never dug into the dirt with your hands and watched a seed spring up through the loam. To see that seasonal reproduction, to participate in your own survival, even just a potted tomato plant on the patio or a kitchen window sill lush and redolent with herbs, is almost primal. After all, God meant us from the beginning to live in an idyllic garden, and surely the longing for that place hasn't left our souls.

We planted our first garden the second summer after we married. As a city slicker, I had a lot to learn. Even my husband Keith, who grew up farming and gardening next door to Jed Clampett, learned that gardens are different in different areas of the country. I suppose I will never forget the time an Illinois brother offered us a bushel of turnips. "Yes!" I replied enthusiastically, then struggled to keep that excited look on my face when he brought me a basket of purple and white roots. In the South we eat the tops, the greens, and throw the roots to the pigs. In the North they do just the opposite. I did learn to cook the things, though I doubt a Northerner would have approved my method. It involved a lot of brown sugar, the only way we could choke them down.

After nearly forty years of gardening, I see why God's prophets and preachers, including Jesus, used so many references to plants and planting—it's only natural. So when it came time for another collection, I had far more gardening devotionals than I needed to fill out a 52 entry book. Here are the best of those. I hope in the next few weeks, or even a year if you spread it out, you will profit from spending a little time in the garden with God.

Dene Ward
March, 2013

In the Garden wtih God

1. Surveying the Garden

As soon as the garden is planted it starts—our evening stroll to see how it fares, what has come up, what is bearing, what is ripe and ready to pick the next morning, which plants show signs of disease or insects, and then, what should we do about it. It's a habit, a ritual almost, one we look forward to every year.

Sometimes I think that God must love gardens too. The first place he built for man, the perfect place, was a garden—"and Jehovah planted a garden, eastward, in Eden, and there he put the man whom he had formed" (Gen 2.8). And it was in that garden that He walked with man every evening. I wonder what they talked about. Probably a lot of the same things we talk about—but then maybe not.

What will be ripe tomorrow? Yes, they might have discussed that, because Eden probably produced a bumper crop. Do we need to spray for bugs? No, not that, for bugs were not a problem. What will be ready for supper tomorrow night? Yes, the choice was probably endless. Do we need to pull the plants that are infected with blight so they won't infect others? No, definitely not that question—at least not at the beginning. Eventually, though, Adam *was* discussing with Eve exactly what we discuss about a far from perfect garden. Yes, we need to spray. Yes, we need to water. Yes, we need to pull those weeds out before they choke out the plants, and I sure hope there's enough produce to put up for next year too!

We each have a garden. The Song of Solomon uses the term to refer to the physical body and chastity. I have no trouble using it to refer to my soul as well. Shouldn't I be out there every evening with God, surveying that garden, examining it for pests and disease, looking for wilt and fungus, making decisions about how to save that garden and make it bear the most fruit for the Lord?

> Examine yourselves, to see whether you are in the faith. Test yourselves. Or do you not realize this about yourselves, that Jesus Christ is in you?—unless indeed you fail to meet the test! (2 Cor 13.5)
>
> Prove me, O LORD, and try me; test my heart and my mind. (Psa 26.2)
>
> Search me, O God, and know my heart! Try me and know my thoughts! And see if there be any grievous way in me, and lead me in the way everlasting! (Psa 139.23–24)

We even sing that last one. Do we mean it? Do we really want to look closely enough to see how to properly tend our gardens, gardens that belong to God? Are we really willing to look through His word long enough and deeply enough to find our faults and fix them?

Every evening God expects you to meet Him in that garden of a soul, to plant His word in it and tend it as necessary, even if it becomes painful. He knows it is the only way for that garden to produce, so that you can someday be in the new Garden of Eden with Him.

> *The righteous flourish like the palm tree and grow like a cedar in Lebanon. They are planted in the house of the LORD; they flourish in the courts of our God. They still bear fruit in old age; they are ever full of sap and green, to declare that the LORD is upright; he is my rock, and there is no unrighteousness in him.*
>
> Psalm 92.12–15

2. Planting from Seed

We plant a lot of tomatoes in our garden. We have learned by trial and error that it is far better to plant more than you think you can possibly use of several different varieties. Some years one type produces better than the others. Some years one will be wiped out by a disease that doesn't touch the others. Usually there is neither rhyme nor reason for any of it. By planting several types, we can be sure to have some, if not all, bear fruit, and by planting too many, if it's a bad year, we still have enough. On the other hand, if it's a good year, we can be generous with friends and neighbors.

We have also learned which types work best in our area. For a long time we could always find what we needed in plants, but gardening has become the fashion now, and just like clothes, certain types of tomatoes are popular. You used to search far and wide for heirlooms. Now you must search far and wide for the ordinary hybrids. The problem with heirlooms, at least in our part of the country, is that they bear about five percent as much as the ordinary hybrid. We usually plant 90–95 tomatoes to fill our needs in canned tomatoes, tomato sauce, and salsa. It isn't so much that we put up a lot; it's that in this heat, tomatoes stop bearing by the end of June. We may have a shorter growing season than our northern neighbors and if we used heirlooms exclusively, we would need to plant nearly 2,000.

If we can't find the reliable varieties of plants in the garden shops any longer, we can find their seeds in at least one of the half dozen seed catalogues we receive. It's a lot more trouble. In our small home, we have to use the entire back bedroom to lay out the seed sponges and set up the grow-lights. When they outgrow the sponges, they are still too small and delicate to place outdoors and the weather still too cold, so we have to transplant each one into a larger cup—all 90, one by one. Then, when the weather finally turns, we have to carry them outside every day, a little longer every day, to harden them for the final transplant into the garden where they will be prey to sun, wind, insects, birds, and animals. Because of our careful preparation, most of them make it. We seldom lose more than half a dozen.

All that because fashion has taken over in gardening instead of common sense and proven track records. It happens in every area of life.

Don't get me started on the organic craze. People had been eating organic foods for thousands of years when Jesus came along and there were still plenty of sick people for him to heal and raise from the dead. Don't tell me they didn't have cancer in those days. Herod the Great is thought to have died of it based upon descriptions of his illness.

Everyone knows how music changes. As far as our songs in the assembled worship, we are seeing a whole lot more rhythm and a whole lot less depth in the words. Or, "Wow!" someone says—usually someone with a music background—"this one actually uses Dorian mode!" Yes, but can an untrained congregation sing it easily enough to focus on the lyrics and actually do some "teaching and admonishing?"

Teaching has its fads. We gave up phonics and wound up with "Johnny Can't Read." In Bible classes we stopped teaching Bible facts to our children because we wanted them to develop the "heart" and not just the knowledge. So now we have ignorant people tearing churches apart over things they should have been taught as children. We used to be known for our Bible knowledge—now many of us are as clueless as any unbeliever on the streets.

Yes, some things are changeable expedients, and I have agreed with most of ours. However, those things should be carefully weighed not only for their rightness, but also for the sake of pure old common sense. Do we want to do it because it will work better for this group of people, or because everyone else is doing it? Some of us wind up planting 2,000 tomatoes just so we look good to the world, when 90 of the right kind would do just fine, probably better, at fulfilling the need.

The seed is the word of God, Jesus said. Maybe it's time we used the seed instead of chasing around looking for something new and exciting. God's way works, but only if you know it, and only if you use it.

Whoever is wise, let him understand these things; whoever is discerning, let him know them; for the ways of the LORD *are right, and the upright walk in them, but transgressors stumble in them.*

Hosea 14.9

3. The Frizzled Tomato Plant

Growing tomatoes can be easy, but if you must deal with poor soil instead of rich loam, it isn't. If you have bacteria-infected soil, it isn't. If blights, mildews, and fungi abound, it isn't. If the insects rise in swarms every time you bump a plant, it isn't. We have all of the above, so growing tomatoes here in our subtropical "paradise" is certainly not easy.

Every year a few of our plants grow to about a foot's height, then stop. Their leaves curl and they never set a bloom. They remain green and don't die outright, but they don't grow and they don't produce fruit. We call them the "frizzled plants" because of the curled leaves and the stunted growth. If we are not careful, our spiritual growth can be stunted in the same way.

Listening and considering new ideas is imperative to spiritual growth, to improving our attitudes and characters. Keith has actually come across a couple of people who have told him, "Even if you could show me in the Bible where I'm wrong, I wouldn't change. I'm comfortable where I am." A comfort zone is prime territory for stunted growth. What do you do but sit there and watch their leaves curl?

Others have a pride issue. They can't possibly be wrong about anything. Hear the sarcasm in Job's voice as he deals with his so-called friends: "No doubt you are the [only wise] people, and wisdom will die with you" (12.2). When people will not listen to anyone else, they will only grow as far as their own knowledge will reach, and then stop.

Parents can stifle growth when they view differing opinions

as disrespect. Even parents who don't mean to do so are used as an excuse not to listen. "But my daddy said..." Don't you think Daddy had enough personal integrity to change his mind if someone showed him he was in error?

Indifference can stunt your growth. In fact, it is a wonder some people managed to germinate a seed at all, much less grow enough to look at least a little like a Christian. Their apathy prevents them from getting any farther.

Wealth can strangle you so that the seed never receives the nourishment it needs. "They are those who hear the word, but the cares of the world and the deceitfulness of riches and the desires for other things enter in and choke the word, and it proves unfruitful" (Mark 4.19).

Immaturity, which Paul repeatedly calls carnality in 1 Corinthians, can stunt your growth. When you are concerned about the wrong things and your perspective is distorted, when you can't see beyond the instant gratification of *things,* status and the opinion of others, you will never comprehend the true necessities of spiritual life. You certainly won't grow in the grace and knowledge of the Lord.

We need to look at ourselves and the things that matter most to us. Examine your spiritual growth in the past year or two. Can you see a difference, or are you still sitting in exactly the same place with curled leaves and no fruit on your limbs? Are you stretching those limbs upward, or do they droop to the earth, where the only things that matter to you happen to be?

What is getting in the way of your growth? Don't be a frizzled tomato plant.

> *Blessed is the man who walks not in the counsel of the wicked, nor stands in the way of sinners, nor sits in the seat of scoffers, but his delight is in the law of Jehovah; And on his law does he meditate day and night. And he shall be like a tree planted by the streams of water, That brings forth its fruit in its season, Whose leaf also doth not wither; And whatever he does shall prosper.*
>
> Psalm 1.1–3

4. Like Tendrils on a Vine

We bought our little piece of acreage nearly 30 years ago, when nothing and no one was back here a half mile off the highway but us. A couple of folks lived up on the main road, and maybe a half dozen within a mile of our turn off, but we were virtually alone because the deeds on the other plots were not yet free and clear for sale. When the boys were growing up, they thought we owned eighty acres, and they roamed it at will.

About eight years later, things changed and a few people moved in. Finally, inevitably I suppose, someone moved next to us. Still, when you are at opposite ends of five acre plots with woods between you, you can pretend you are alone. Then the folks "next door" moved their married children to the back of their five acres, and suddenly we had a neighbor about two hundred feet across the fence, way too close by our standards.

Then they cleared out the pine trees, and some of the brush went down under the heavy equipment too. I feel like I am on display now, especially at night, since their front door faces our front windows. They would still need binoculars to see anything, but that doesn't make me feel a bit better.

So last spring we built a twelve foot high trellis and planted a combination of confederate jasmine, purple trumpet flowers, blue passion vines, and Carolina jessamine to screen us. By next summer it should be doing a pretty good job of that. The tendrils of one jasmine, a couple of the Jessamines, and all the passions vines have already wound their way up to the top of the trellis. All of them are well-established with new shoots sprouting all over the runners, and all nine plants have even bloomed this year, which we never expected after their being transplanted.

I was reading Proverbs 14 the other day and came across this one in verse 3: "By the mouth of a fool comes a rod for his pride." I just assumed it was a rod of correction, as in "He who spares the rod spoils his child." I don't know what made me look up "rod" in the concordance, but I am glad I did because I made a discovery. This word is not the same word usually translated "rod." In fact, it is only found one other time in the Bible, in Isaiah 11.1: "And there shall come forth a shoot out of the stock of Jesse, and a branch out of his roots shall bear fruit."

The word translated rod in that Proverbs passage is not "stock" and it is not "branch." It is "shoot," as in a leaf sprouting out of a main branch. That gives you a whole new insight into the proverb.

When a fool talks, those words are shooting forth from the main branch—his pride. They are a product of arrogance, conceit, and self-satisfaction. It may not be that a person who talks a lot is always a proud person, but it is certainly true that a proud person talks too much. He is busy trying to convince everyone else that he is as good as he thinks he is.

Now think about those vines of ours. Once the tendrils catch hold of the trellis they are tenacious. It is nearly impossible to get them loose without breaking a branch. Even if you cut the plant at the bottom, the vine will hang on for several days, and if it has been close to something organic—the ground, the branch of another plant—it may very well have rooted on its own and just keep climbing.

When your pride starts branching out, its tendrils will wind around to the point that it is nearly impossible to get it out of your system. Maybe that is why it is one of the things God especially warns us about. You cannot fix your problems when you cannot see them, and pride will blind you to your own faults as nothing else can.

I want the vines on my trellis to screen me from my neighbors, but you don't want a vine that screens you from any correction your soul desperately needs. Be careful when you find yourself talking a lot. It might be sprouting from pride, and once that pride catches hold of you, your soul is in grave danger.

> *Talk no more so exceeding proudly; let not arrogance come out of your mouth. For Jehovah is a God of knowledge, and by him actions are weighed.*
>
> 1 Samuel 2.3

5. Periwinkle Wilt

My grandmother grew periwinkles in the small space between the sidewalk on Main Street and her front porch. They bloomed every year without fail, spilling over on to the walkway by the end of summer, pink, purple, lilac, white, and magenta blossoms, paper-thin petals flourishing in the hot Florida sun. She never replanted, they simply reappeared every year like clockwork, and multiplied as the years passed.

So when I needed an easy plant to fill a raised bed in the front of the house, one that would reseed and gradually mulch itself, I naturally thought of periwinkles, or vinca as they are now called. Imagine my disappointment when one by one they began to wilt and die, regardless the watering or fertilizing.

With a little effort I found websites mentioning "periwinkle wilt." Unfortunately, there were as many theories about the causes as there were websites, and no one had a solution. One "expert" suggested growing them only in the winter, implying that the wilt was caused by the heat, in direct opposition to my own experiences with the plant as a child. If anything, central Florida is hotter than north Florida, and they grew fine down there, even surrounded with hot concrete in the middle of town. Besides, North Florida winters would kill them. We have far too many frosts and freezes.

I finally managed to get a few of the plants to live last summer, not through my own efforts, but more the luck of the draw, I think. This year I tried again with more than a little trepidation. Sure enough they started dying, even faster than last year's, and even more of them. But lo and behold, there in between my wilting new plants rose seedlings spawned by the few survivors last year. I carefully tended them, watering and fertilizing, and they are blooming now, with absolutely no signs of wilt at all.

Why should that surprise me so? Who will do the best job, the one who enjoys his work, or the one you practically have to stand over with a whip? We call plants that spring up from seed "volunteers." God has always wanted "volunteers." If He had wanted robots that would do everything exactly as He wanted it to be done, He would have made them. What He wanted were people who volunteer, who, out of their own free will, without being forced to, will worship and serve Him. Wouldn't you?

The scriptures make a distinction between things done voluntarily and those done "from compulsion." Even from the time of the Old Law God instituted free will offerings that had nothing to do with the minimum requirements (Num 15.3). Under the New we are to give as we have "purposed," "not reluctantly or under compulsion, for God loves a cheerful giver" (2 Cor 9.7). The elders are told to "shepherd the flock… not under compulsion, but willingly" (1 Pet 5.2). Romans 12 gives us a whole list of things to do for one another, things that grow out of the great teaching Paul has done in the first 8 chapters of the book. Notice how we are to do those things: contribute "with generosity; lead with zeal"; perform acts of mercy "with cheerfulness" (12.8). Could it be any clearer that these are to be voluntary actions?

This must all stem from a voluntary decision to become a disciple of Christ. If that is not the basis of it all, the rest will never happen. If I became a Christian because my parents expected it, because I wanted to marry someone, because my little sister "went forward" before I did, because I was caught up in an emotional situation and I wanted to be like everyone else (think "summer Bible camp"), did I really make a voluntary, reasoned decision to commit the rest of my life to God no matter what the cost?

When you volunteer for something, it is much easier to see it through. Even when the task becomes more difficult than you ever imagined, the commitment borne of love or passion to the cause will keep you going. Volunteers will last. Hot house flowers will wilt in the heat.

Perhaps it is time to question your original motives, your original decision and the mindset that led to it. Perhaps it is time to really volunteer, rather than just going through the motions out of a motive far less important than a sincere desire to worship your Creator.

> *And as for you, son of man, the children of your people talk of you by the walls and in the doors of the houses, and speak one to another, every one to his brother, saying, Come, I pray you, and hear what is the word that comes forth from Jehovah. And they come to you* **as** *the people come, and they sit before you* **as** *my people, and they hear your words, but do them not; for with their mouth they show much love, but their heart goes after their gain. And, lo, you are to them as a very lovely song of one that has a pleasant voice, and can play well on an instrument; for they hear your words, but they do them not.*
>
> Ezekiel 33.30–32

6. Count Your Blossoms

Since late last year it has begun to look like things are on a downward trend. Before long there may very well be more surgeries, even riskier than before. I usually cope fairly well, but one morning the blues hit particularly hard. I was out with Chloe and came upon the morning glories. We saw more blooms that day than any before, at least five shades of blue and purple, and a lilac-throated white as well.

Why I did it, I don't know, but I began assigning names to each blossom, names of people who have been special blessings to me during this journey toward blindness. At first I thought I would run out of names before I ran out of blooms. Higher and higher my eyes roamed, spotting another and another, and yet another bloom ten feet above the ground. When I ran out of blooms I still had a dozen names left over.

Suddenly my steps became springier and my mood brightened. Look how many people have been there for me, driving me all over, picking up medications for me, sending cards, calling, bringing meals, giving me an encouraging word, and often a hug, even helping me with some of the earlier expenses that the insurance company wouldn't touch, and always praying.

"My grace is sufficient," Jesus told Paul when he had prayed for the thorn to be removed. "It doesn't need to be removed; you just have to trust that I will help you through it." He has certainly given me ample help.

Too many times, instead of looking up to count the blooms, I am looking down to count the weeds. Do you know what?

There were far more blooms than weeds that morning, and it is so in my life as well. In fact, some of those blooms once were weeds, but through the grace of the Lord working in our lives, the two of us managed to make a new relationship that we both count as blooms now. In some cases, the grace that made this happen were the very trials we prayed to have removed.

So today, as you walk through your life's garden, don't look down and count the weeds. Look up and count the blossoms that hang from the vine of Christ's grace, the grace He promised would help you overcome, would make you stronger, and would cover any weaknesses you still might have after giving your all. Put a name on every one of those blossoms. I imagine you will have names left over too, names you forget about when your mind stays too long in the weeds, people who have made the hard times easier to bear, and who will hold you up when life beats too hard for you to stand on your own.

God is the reason those blooms are there, as He sheds yet more grace into your life, promising that nothing will happen that is too hard for you to bear, and that you will never have to bear it alone.

> *Fear not for I am with you; be not dismayed for I am your God; I will strengthen you, I will help you; I will uphold you with my righteous right hand.*
>
> Isaiah 41.10

7. Mulch

Keith decided that since we have gone to so much trouble and spent so much money on this trellis with nine vining plants, a raised bed and 36 periwinkles clustered at the base of the vines, that we should mulch it properly. So he bought 12 bags of cypress mulch. I am thrilled. I have already spent more time weeding this thing than I did the whole vegetable garden this year, and the other morning just as I was getting close to the purple trumpet flower a snake crawled out of it. I will be happy not to have to stick my face down so close to that vine in the future.

We often use the metaphor of weeds choking out a person's spirituality. "And he that was sown among the thorns, this is he who hears the word, and the care of the world and the deceitfulness of riches, choke the word and he becomes unfruitful" (Matt 13.22)—certainly a good and scriptural analogy. We had a little problem with that in our beans this year as a matter of fact.

But if weeds growing up around a plant can choke it out, certainly a four inch layer of mulch lying around the plant can choke the weeds out. If we fill our lives with righteousness, with service to others, and with God's word, sin won't have a chance.

One reason weeds will choke out a plant is that they steal the nutrients out of the ground. They steal the water. They steal the sunlight by growing over the plants and shading them. A good layer of mulch will steal those same things from the weeds. They will not be able to grow, and meanwhile the good plants will become stronger and larger. The mulch also keeps the ground cooler and retains moisture, creating a better environment for the plant. If a weed somehow does manage to find a crack through which to grow, the plant won't die from it, and it is so obvious it will be pulled immediately.

Mulch your life today, "being filled with the fruits of righteousness which are through Jesus Christ, unto the glory and praise of God" (Phil 1.11). Surround yourself with good people who will encourage you and teach you, who will set good examples, and whose needs will keep you so busy serving you don't have time for sin. Spend time with the word of God, reading, studying, attending Bible classes, and listening to sermons. Pray as often as you can, not just before bed and at meals. Cram so much righteousness into your life that no room remains for anything else. Then watch how seldom you sin and how much you grow, less of the one and more of the other than ever before.

> *For this cause we also, since the day we heard, do not cease to pray and make request for you, that you may be filled with the knowledge of his will in all spiritual wisdom and understanding to walk worthily of the Lord unto all pleasing, bearing fruit in every good work, and increasing in the knowledge of God; strengthened with all power, according to the might of his glory unto all patience and longsuffering with joy.*
>
> Colossians 1.9–11

8. Parsley Worms

I had just checked the day before. How could this be? The herbed rice pilaf was simmering on the stove, and I had run out to the herb garden to cut some parsley to add just before serving. Five healthy Italian flat leaf parsley plants were stripped bare. I leaned to look closer and there they were—four black and green striped parsley worms. They may well have been there the day before, hidden by the bushy leaves, and their green color, the same shade as the parsley stems, but to me it was as if they had eaten them all overnight.

Luckily, the butter, onions, garlic, chicken broth, thyme and toasted almonds gave the pilaf a little flavor at least, and the rest of the meal turned out fine. Enough sauce covered the cider-braised pork chops so that anyone desiring to could spoon it over the rice as well. But it was still missing those pretty flecks of green and the freshness that a good-sized handful of fresh parsley added at the last minute brings. If only I had looked a little closer the day before, even I might have seen those little stinkers.

It can happen to us as easily as to parsley plants. False teachers are charming, logical, and usually attractive people. They will appeal to your sense of justice, common sense, compassion, ego, even your pocketbook, whatever it takes to get your attention and draw you in. Many of them sincerely believe what they teach, having been previously deceived by yet another false teacher. Those are especially difficult to ignore—what seems like an honest and sincere person cannot be the evil wolf Jesus warns us about, can he? "And no marvel; for even Satan fashions himself into an angel of light. It is no great thing therefore if his ministers also fashion themselves as ministers of righteousness..." (2 Cor 11.14–15).

So whose fault is it if we are taken in by these people? God makes it clear in both the Old and New Testaments that we are responsible for our own souls.

> A wonderful and a horrible thing has come to pass in the land. The prophets prophesy falsely and the priests bear rule by their means, *and my people love to have it so.* (Jer 5.30–31)

> For it is a rebellious people, lying children, *children that will not hear the law of the Jehovah,* that say to the Seers, see not, and to the Prophets, prophesy not right things, but *speak to us smooth things.* (Isa 30.9–10)

> For the time will come when they will not endure sound doctrine, but, *having itching ears, will heap to themselves teachers after their own lusts, and will turn away their ears from the truth and turn aside unto fables.* (2 Tim 4.3–4)

Scary, isn't it? Don't think it cannot happen to you and, like my parsley plants, happen quickly. Before the apostles were dead, the first "-ism" was already upon the church. They were fighting the Judaizing brethren, the Gnostics, the Nicolaitans, and others we probably will never know about.

"I am astonished that you are so quickly deserting him who called you in the grace of Christ and are turning to a different gospel, not that there is another one, but there are some who trouble you and want to distort the gospel of Christ," Paul told the Galatians (1.6–7), not 20 years after founding the churches in that area. How about us two thousand years removed? If there was ever a time for vigilance, for going back to the basics, for attempting to restore the New Testament church as God intended it to be, it is now. So many have strayed so far.

When your elders and preachers seem harsh and intolerant toward a teacher or group, or even toward you, give them a break. Your souls are in their hands. They are seeing things that you, caught up in your emotions and prejudices, might not. Like parents protecting a child from the predators out there in the world, they can see the danger. Instead of adolescently complaining, "You're mean. You don't understand," pay attention. Ultimately, if you choose not to listen to them, the parsley worms will eat up your souls, leaving nothing but useless stems, and God will hold *you* accountable.

> *Beware of false prophets who come to you in sheep's clothing, but inwardly are ravenous wolves. You will recognize them by their fruits.*
>
> *Beloved, do not believe every spirit, but test the spirits to see whether they are from God, for many false prophets have gone out into the world.*
>
> Matthew 7.15–16; 1 John 4.1

9. A Pepper By Any Other Name

Garden season is in full swing down here in Florida. Last month I transplanted my herb seedlings from cups to the herb bed. We made the first transplant in March from the peat plugs we had placed the seeds in, to larger cups. We always write the type of plant on the cup so if they get mixed up, we will know what we are working with. Some of the cups were clear plastic and the dark potting soil made it difficult to read the black marker writing on the outside. Yet I could see "Sweet Ba" and since the majority of the plugs were herbs, I was positive they were "sweet basil" plants.

Imagine my surprise when, after planting the plants, I picked up two of the now empty clear cups and was able to see "Sweet Banana" on the side. Two of those five plants were banana peppers, not basil! So I dug those two out and took them to the main garden, transplanting them yet again, this time into the pepper row. I double-checked all the cups, and yes, there were only two. The others were either Sweet Basil or Marseilles Basil.

That evening as I showed Keith the herb bed and told him the story, he walked around and looked at the basil from a different angle. "You know," he said, "those three plants look like peppers too."

"Impossible," I told him. "I was very careful when we transplanted them to write what each plant was on the outside, and those are basil!" Besides, I thought to myself, you are a vegetable gardener, not an herbalist. You don't even know what half these things are.

Then I leaned a little closer—well, actually a lot closer. Those leaves *were* a little different, a bit more spade-shaped, but then French basil looks much different than Italian too. Finally I reached down and rubbed a leaf between my thumb and forefinger, and lifted them to my nose. I should have been knocked over by the strong smell of basil. Instead I got maybe a little whiff of "green" smell, nothing more. They were indeed pepper plants.

I wonder how many times we are too sure of ourselves. We know what we know, we know how we got that knowledge, and we know that we know more than most, so how can we be wrong? We have believed this thing for years. Our parents or some highly respected teacher taught us. It cannot possibly be wrong.

So there we sit with peppers in our herb bed. Peppers are good to have. I cook with them a lot. But when it comes time for a Caprese salad they are totally out of place, and I would like to see anyone try to make pesto with them. Even if I am positive they are basil, the facts won't change, and I will simply look ignorant to those with unbiased vision.

Don't get too sure of yourself. Be willing to listen. Be willing to double-check anything and anyone, including, and most especially perhaps, yourself.

> *The Almighty—we cannot find him; he is great in power; justice and abundant righteousness he will not violate. Therefore men fear him; he does not regard any who are wise in their own conceit.*
>
> Job 37.23–24

10. Growing Basil

I have had a terrible time with my basil this year. It will not grow. It just sits there exactly the same height and with the same number of leaves, day after day. Usually, even though I use it a lot, it becomes a shrub, and I must cut four cups at a time making pesto every couple of weeks to keep up with it. This year I had to ration it in things like my orzo salad with grape tomatoes, green onions, pine nuts, feta, and basil, and the cherry tomato salad with basil, fresh mozzarella, garlic, and balsamic vinegar. Pesto was not even in the forecast, and my late summer marinara may be blander than it has ever been before.

Basil is one of the easiest herbs to grow. Being Mediterranean, it can take the Florida heat and humidity. It may wilt on a hot summer afternoon, but recovers quickly in the evening and looks like new the next morning. It can handle the worst of circumstances. It doesn't even have its own particular pest like parsley has parsley worms. So what is the problem this year? We watered it during the dry weather and fertilized it as usual. I have no idea what happened. Maybe I took it for granted that it was a strong plant needing no special care.

Strong Christians can be like that. People get so used to them being strong that no one checks on them, no one asks how things are going, no one gives them an encouraging word—that's what *they* are supposed to do.

When was the last time you patted an elder on the back and thanked him for his work, maybe even apologized for any trouble or worry you might have caused him? When was the last time you sent him a note or a card of appreciation? How about his wife? She must not only deal with some of the same problems he does, but watch the effect of it all on him—distress etching lines in his face, frustration turning his hair gray a bit too early, his smile all but disappearing over the sorrow for lost souls.

How about the preacher? Even people who don't mean anything by it can say hurtful things, can judge harshly, and can expect the impossible—perfection. Preachers and their wives must watch their children grow up too early as they see their father mistreated over and over, everywhere they go. It's a wonder any of them stay faithful.

The worst thing you can do to a strong Christian is tell him or her that you know he is strong and can take anything. Sometimes they can't. Sometimes it just gets to be too much, and instead of having brethren who will pull them out of the abyss, they must climb out all by themselves because no one thinks they need any help.

Find a strong Christian today and do them a favor—forget they are strong. Treat them as if they needed a boost and then give them one. They will appreciate it more than you can imagine.

> *[And Jehovah said] Charge* ***Joshua*** *and* ***encourage him and strengthen him****, for he shall go over before this people and he shall cause them to inherit this land which you shall see.*
>
> Deuteronomy 3.28

> *Wherefore brethren, exhort one another and build each other up, even as you also do. But we beseech you brethren, know* ***those who labor among you****, and are over you in the Lord, and who admonish you.* ***to esteem them highly in love for their work's sake.***
>
> 1 Thessalonians 5.11–13

> [**Paul** *said,*] *Finally brethren,* ***pray for us****.*
>
> 2 Thessalonians 3.1

11. Wildflowers

We love this season. You never know what will pop up where.

Several years ago we started planting wildflowers, a patch here one year and a patch there the next, babying them for exactly one summer, then letting them do their own thing. Every spring we eagerly await the results. Last year black-eyed Susans sprang up where we had never planted them. This year rain lilies rose in a larger clump and farther from the original bed than you would have thought possible. The year before a bright yellow coreopsis suddenly bloomed way out in the field amid nothing but grass. It's exciting to see what can happen over the years from just one seed sown in the middle of five acres.

I have had the same experience lately with my old Bible class literature. Suddenly I received a drop ship order from one of the Bible book stores to an address nearly 2,000 miles distant. Yet the last name, an uncommon one especially considering the relatively small size of the brotherhood, was familiar. It was the first name I didn't know. Was this the daughter, or maybe the daughter-in-law of a woman I taught thirty years ago? Imagine that.

Don't you think the apostles had the same feelings when, years after they had sown the seed in a rough Gentile town, they had news of another group of disciples, or maybe several groups, in the same vicinity? The power of God's word screams out from the growth of the church in the ancient world and the way it changed history itself.

I have had people who knew my parents in their younger

years tell me of the things they did for them, things they still remembered and that obviously meant a lot. Keith has had people come up to him and say, "I still have that letter you wrote me years ago. It changed my life." And, "I remember that class you taught. It helped me through a rough time."

We have opportunities every day to make a difference in someone's life. Too many times we ignore them because we don't believe anything we say or do will make that much difference. Let me tell you something. It isn't yourself you are demeaning by thinking that way—it's God's word and His power through that word. When you help someone, when you speak a word of encouragement, when you act with kindness in a situation where no one else would have bothered, you are tapping into that power yourself and spreading the grace of God to others. It may be just the "cup of cold water" Jesus mentions in Matthew 10.42, but that cup can change a life.

I have lost count of the times people have said to me, "I remember when you..." You know what? Most of the time, I *don't* remember it, but I thank God for sending some small amount of inspiration for me to say the right thing, even though I was perfectly oblivious at the time. Truly He helps us in every circumstance.

When our lives are over, we should be able to walk out into the field and find little patches of grace that came from some seed we sowed, however inadvertently, years before. Yellow daisies, white rain lilies, blue bachelors' buttons, pink phlox, red cypress vines—you never know what you will get when you spread the word with an act of kindness or word of compassion—*no matter how small it may seem to you!*

So put on your gardening gloves this morning and start planting.

> *For as the rain and the snow come down from heaven and do not return there but water the earth, making it bring forth and sprout, giving seed to the sower and bread to the eater, so shall my word be that goes out from my mouth; it shall not return to*

me empty, but it shall accomplish that which I purpose, and shall succeed in the thing for which I sent it.

Isaiah 55.10–11

12. Spiderworts

We kept seeing them on the side of the road—two to three feet high, blue flowers clustered at the top of tall stems with long narrow leaves. We called them wild irises because that's what they looked like, and I wished aloud that we had some. So Keith stopped one afternoon on the way home from work and dug up a few. I looked them up in my wildflower book and found their true name—spiderwort. What an ugly name, I thought, and called them my wild irises instead.

Then we learned about them. They spread faster than anything we had ever planted, in places we really didn't want them, but the worst was this—they were only beautiful early in the morning or right after a rain. Otherwise those blooms turned black and ugly by noon, earlier in the heat of summer. If ever there was a fair weather flower, this was it.

Just as I misjudged the beauty of those wildflowers, I fear that some of us may be mistaken about how God judges our beauty. Dressing up on Sunday morning is not what matters to God. Having a tie on is not what makes a man worthy to serve at the Lord's Table. While I dress carefully on Sundays, one of the few times I get to wear a pretty dress these days, it has little to do with whether God thinks I am beautiful. To God, beauty is seen in faithfulness, in righteous and holy lives, and in kindness shown to others. In many cases, we don't look particularly pretty while doing those things.

We never look better to God than when we are bruised and bloody from a fight with Satan, battered from overcoming the temptation to sin. We are pretty when we are clad in old clothes cleaning up after our families, and handsome when plastered with sweat and dirt from doing the yard work for a widow. We are lovely to God when we sit around in our old blue jeans talking about the Bible to a friend who asked a question, or inviting a neighbor to a Bible study. We are beautiful to Him when our bodies are thin and our eyes sunken from facing an illness that came only because so many years ago the Devil succeeded with Adam, yet we face it with trust in a God who has a plan. We are especially gorgeous to Him when our bodies are old and bent, and our hair gray and thin, having lived a life of faithfulness.

Spiderworts are pretty only when things are easy, only when life is fun. When that's over, they live up to their name—black and ugly, a weed everyone could do without. Don't make God feel that way about you.

> *I am faint and sore bruised: I have groaned because of the tumult of my heart. Lord, all my desire is before you; And my groaning is not hidden from you. My heart throbs, my strength fails me: As for the light of mine eyes, it also is gone from me. My lovers and my friends stand aloof from my plague; And my kinsmen stand afar off… in you, O Jehovah, do I hope: You will answer, O Lord my God.*
>
> Psalm 38.8–11, 15

13. Lessons Learned Down on My Knees: Focus

The vegetable garden has taken all my time lately and the flower beds are showing it. A few days ago I started the weeding, content to make a quarter "pie slice" in the circular morning glory bed. The next day I took forty-five minutes out of my morning to finish.

The vines were doing fine once they got to the trellis, climbing over 12 feet high by now and blooming every morning, but the bed itself was ankle high not only in morning glories but also moneywort, wood sorrel, snake root, castor beans, and purslane, among other colorfully named weeds, plus a little grass as well. I started with the previous day's pie slice, amazed that so many of those rascals had once again sprung up overnight, but that was easily handled in about five minutes.

I learned some things as I spent the time kneeling in the damp grass. First, whenever you get down on their level, the dogs think you are ready to play. Instantly the two of them were at my elbows, tails wagging, inundating me with doggy breath, and grunting for my time and affection. So I gave them a few requisite pats, hugs, and praises as I meandered away from the bed before they could decide to throw themselves on their backs in the middle of it, begging for a belly rub.

Finally they were satisfied and I started pulling weeds in earnest. With my diminished vision I have to concentrate to see what I am doing. I finished up another slice and stood up to catch my breath and my equilibrium. When I looked back down I could hardly believe my eyes. I thought I just weeded that section, but no, all I had done was pull up the moneywort. The wood sorrel was still there, wiggling its little leaves at me in what I was sure was smug satisfaction. So I bent once again and pulled it all up. When I finished I sat back on my haunches and looked it over. Now I saw the snake root, not much of it to be sure, but it was odd that I had not seen it at all when it was by far the tallest weed in the bed.

Suddenly I made sense of it all. I had to focus so hard to see one thing I was blinding myself to the others. I looked for more of the taller plants and there were the rest of the snakeroots as if they were waving a flag at me saying, "Here we are!" Then I looked for the purslanes' creeping red stems and shiny green leaves and there they were, ready for the pulling. Then the castor beans, and the cow vetch, and the grass—well, you get the point. You will only see what you are looking for.

Do you wonder why you cannot see your own faults? Maybe it is because you are focused on everyone else's.

Do you wonder why you are so stressed about life? Maybe it is because you are too focused on it—on paying the bills, handling the schedules, dealing with work problems—and not focused on the things that really matter. Jesus tells us in more than one passage that focus on the wrong things can cost us our souls.

Are you so focused on your own problems that you cannot see the problems of others? Maybe that is why you are so down in the dumps all the time.

On the other hand, do you focus so much on your own failures that you cannot see your successes? Maybe you have grown by leaps and bounds in the past few years. You will never know it if all you do is tear yourself up over today's failures. Guess what? Tomorrow morning I will have to pull a few more weeds from that morning glory bed, but I doubt it will take 45 minutes. The fact that a few grew back does not mean I should never have bothered to pull them all in the first place.

Work on your focus today. Train yourself in what to look for. Make sure you are seeing the things you need to see, rather than the things you want to see. You will never reach a point where there are no weeds to pull, but you can totally eradicate some and make the others far less common.

> *For if these things [faith, virtue, knowledge, self-control, patience, godliness, brotherly kindness, love] are yours and abound, they make you to be neither idle nor unfruitful unto the knowledge of our Lord Jesus Christ. For he who lacks these things is blind, seeing only what is near, having forgotten the cleansing from his old sins. Wherefore brethren, give the more diligence to make your calling and election sure; for if you do these things, you shall never stumble, for thus shall be richly supplied unto you the entrance into the eternal kingdom of our Lord and Savior Jesus Christ.*
>
> 2 Peter 1.8–11

14. Lessons Learned Down on My Knees: Direction

As I worked my way around that morning glory bed, I discovered some interesting things. We had originally planted the seeds in concentric circles, and then as the vines grew we trained them to head to the center of the bed toward the huge metal trellis, a cow panel Keith had woven along half an old antenna pole and then stood up on its end toward the sky, fifteen feet high. Every year they come back, but they aren't in circles any longer. They grow up wherever the seeds fall from the dried out blooms the year before. The more weeds I pulled, the better I could see the vines, and a few surprises awaited me.

More than once I had to be careful not to pull out a morning glory along with the weed. The long spindly vines often clung to the weeds, and I had to carefully unwind them. Sometimes as I unwound them I discovered that they were headed in the wrong direction—to the outer edge of the circle rather than toward the trellis. These I carefully turned around until they were pointing the right way.

Other times the vine was too tightly wound around the weed, using it as a trellis, despite the fact that it was nestled, supposedly safely, among its brother vines. The only way I could get it loose was to break it off. Those I was especially careful with, laying them along the ground pointing toward the true trellis, and watering them deeply. Maybe they will survive and maybe not, but the only hope they had was the amputation. Maybe they will live but their growth be stunted. Maybe they will mend and grow again. Time will tell and we all know that healing often hurts.

And then there were the morning glories I found totally outside the bed, headed in no direction at all. What to do? Well, I guess I could have picked up a spade and a hoe and made the bed large enough to include them, but that would have been ridiculous unless we eventually wanted our whole yard to be one morning glory patch. So I pulled a few, the ones that looked iffy to begin with, and transplanted others. Will they live? I don't know, but they would have been mown down next weekend if I had done nothing.

Another thing I discovered underneath all those weeds was new morning glories. Some vines were only a couple of inches long. But now they will have a chance. They will not be choked out by the weeds that steal the nutrients from the soil and shade the sun. New growth cannot happen if you don't get rid of those weeds.

Spend a few moments today thinking about the metaphors here. Are you clinging to something besides the Lord? Have you wandered away from His care? Are you trying to make His flower bed bigger than He made it? And, ultimately, are you headed in the right direction, toward the one trellis that reaches for the sky?

> *And he answered and said, He who sows the good seed is the Son of man, and the field is the world, and the good seed, these are the sons of the kingdom; and the weeds are the sons of the evil one; and the enemy that sowed them is the devil; and the harvest is the end of the world, and the reapers are the angels. As therefore the weeds are gathered up and burned with fire, so shall it be in the end of the world.*
>
> Matthew 13.37–40

15. Lessons Learned Down on My Knees: The Underground

When you pull up any sort of plant by the roots, you are likely to pull up some soil as well, and often some wigglers you never knew were there.

As I pulled up the more deeply rooted weeds around those morning glories, I often pulled up a few earthworms. Earthworms are a good sign. They work to cultivate the soil and leave it well fertilized. Generally speaking, the more earthworms you find, the better your crop and the prettier your flowers. But a few times I pulled up some ugly stuff—things that were not beneficial to the plants, things that would feed on the roots, and eventually kill them.

I couldn't help but think of the "underground" among God's people. I think one of the most comforting things to know is that there are a few earthworms out there in the garden, good people quietly seeing to the things they can, visiting, calling, advising, teaching, and in the process defusing a few bombs before anyone even knows they are there. They take care of the minor problems so the elders have the time to deal with the major ones. In fact, because of their work, some of the major problems never come to pass. They don't worry about not getting their fair share of attention from those men either. They are spiritually mature enough not to need constant coddling.

On the other hand, there might very well be a few uglies underground, roiling the waters, attempting to stir up controversy and dissatisfaction. They often disguise themselves as earthworms, "just trying to make people think," "playing Devil's Advocate so we can get a helpful dialogue going." Those sorts of dialogues need a carefully chosen audience. Instead of being careful of the babes who may not be ready for such a discussion, they are often actively seeking to turn their vulnerable minds from the simple Truth of the Gospel toward themselves and their own pet beliefs. At best, they are careless of the souls of others. When the church must take its attention away from its mission of saving the lost in order to pander to the egos of the bitter and undo the carelessness of the inconsiderate, the Devil does indeed have an advocate, and he is in control. The more minions he has working underground, the fewer lost souls will be reached, and the fewer saved ones will make it to the end of the road.

Think about that the next time you have a conversation, either in the church or with a lost soul out in the world. What just reared its head above the soil line? Did it help a soul find the Lord, or did it raise antipathy toward the body for which Christ died? Whose side are you working for?

> *Now I beseech you brethren, mark those who are causing divisions and occasions of stumbling contrary to the doctrine which you learned, and turn away from them. For they who are such serve not our Lord Jesus Christ, but their own bellies, and by their smooth and fair speech, they beguile the hearts of the innocent.*
>
> Romans 16.17–18

16. Up Close and Personal

I had an up close and personal encounter with a wildflower a couple of weeks ago. When we plant a new bed out in the field, we baby it the first year. The point is for them to grow up scattered in the grasses and among other wildflowers in a natural way, but if you don't get them off to a good start, they won't stand a chance with all the competition out there for ground space and rainwater.

So I was weeding the latest patch, which we had let go far beyond the normal time span. I had difficulty even finding some of the small plants amid all the waist high grass and weeds. I had nearly finished, was soaking wet and black up to my elbows, when I noticed one more low-growing weed and bent over to pull it. I did not see the bare stalk of the wildflower right between my feet, leafless and flowerless, standing three feet high. I did not know it was there until, as I bent over, it slid right into my eye like a hot wire. Which eye? The one which most lately has been operated on, the one with the shunt, the capsular tension ring, and the silicone lens, the one that already hurts the most.

The doctor and I spent nearly two weeks fixing me up after this little mishap, checking to see if there was any permanent damage, checking to see if the shunt had been knocked out of place, checking for infection, and worse, for plant fungus. As it turns out, all I had was a hematoma and a laceration, but it was an exciting couple of weeks.

That was too close and personal an encounter with a flower, but we can never be too close and personal with God. I have had to learn that. The prevailing sentiment many years ago seemed to be that we did not want to do or say anything that might make someone apply a religious pejorative to us indicating belief in something other than correct Bible teaching about God, Christ, and the Holy Spirit. Instead of saying, "I'm blessed," instead of saying, "God took care of me," indeed, instead of attributing anything to the providence of God, we said, "I'm lucky." We wouldn't want someone to get the wrong idea, would we?

Where did we come up with that? Read some of David's psalms. He gave God the credit for everything. Read Hannah's song, or Moses and Miriam's after crossing the Red Sea. Since when don't the people of God tell everyone what God has done for them?

Read some of Paul's sermons. He does not seem a bit concerned that someone might use what he says to give credence to false teaching. "You know that idol you have out there?" he asks the Athenians, "the one to the Unknown God? Let me tell you about him." He tells Felix, "But this I confess to you that after the Way which they call a sect, so serve I the God of our fathers" (Acts 24.14). It didn't matter a bit what people called it, as long as he could talk about it. In fact, he used their misconceptions as opportunities to preach the Gospel.

Maybe that is my problem—I don't want to talk about it. It makes me uncomfortable. It has nothing to do with whether someone gets the wrong idea about the Truth, but everything to do with me feeling ill at ease, or downright embarrassed. I don't want to be called a religious fanatic and certainly not a "Holy Roller!" Yes, I want a close, personal relationship with God, as long as no one else knows about it.

But here is the deal: If I am too embarrassed by my relationship with God to even acknowledge it, then He won't acknowledge me either, and *I* am the one with everything to lose.

Go out there today and say or do something that will make someone else curious enough to ask you a question. Then open your mouth and unashamedly tell them how wonderful an up close and personal relationship with your Creator and Savior really is.

> *Everyone therefore who shall confess me before men, him will I also confess before my Father who is in Heaven. But whoever shall deny me before men, him will I also deny before my Father who is in Heaven.*
>
> Matthew 10.32–33

17. Putting Down Roots

Keith's mother once gave him a tiny orange tree, maybe six inches tall, which she had planted from seed into a coffee can. He brought it home, transplanted it into a black plastic nursery pot and set it next to the shed, continuing to water and feed it until he could find a permanent place for it.

It had grown to a height of three feet when he finally decided where to put it. Bending down, he grabbed the pot with both hands and tugged. Nothing happened. The tree had made its own decision, its roots bursting through the bottom of the pot and digging their way firmly into the ground. It's still there, now over twice as tall as the shed and bearing fruit nearly year round.

Our children are like that little tree. Wherever you leave them is where they will put down roots. The atmosphere you raise them in, the people they spend the most time with, the friends they make and the activities they participate in, whether you are aware of them or not, will all have their effects on your children and will influence who they eventually become.

Children are growing every minute of every day, not only in body, but also in mind. You cannot set them aside until you have more time, you cannot leave them on their own without guidance, you cannot give them into the charge of another whose belief system does not match yours and still expect your children to follow in your footsteps. You cannot tell them, not even with all the sincerity you can muster, "Just wait till I finish this degree; just wait till my career is more established; just wait till I can pay off all these bills I ran up, then I will be a good parent to you." If nothing else, you are teaching them exactly what is most important to you—career, status, "things." Meanwhile, they may put down their roots in places you wish they never knew of, with people you wish they had never met, and develop a character that may appall you.

"Where did they learn that?" you might wonder. In the place where you left them while you were too busy to be a parent.

Unless the LORD builds the house,
those who build it labor in vain.
Unless the LORD watches over the city,
the watchman stays awake in vain.
It is in vain that you rise up early
and go late to rest,
eating the bread of anxious toil;
for he gives to his beloved sleep.
Behold, children are a heritage from the LORD,
the fruit of the womb a reward.
Like arrows in the hand of a warrior
are the children of one's youth.
Blessed is the man
who fills his quiver with them!
He shall not be put to shame
when he speaks with his enemies in the gate.

Psalm 127

18. Pot-bound

In our quest to diligently teach our children, I think we often overlook something. We care for our children, nurturing both body and soul. Our task, though, is to work our way out of the job. If my thirty year old child still cannot dress himself, or needs to be reminded to brush his teeth, I have failed miserably. In the same way, our children cannot make it to Heaven on our spiritual coattails.

It is often difficult for a parent to realize that his child's faith should be his own, not an exact replica of his. A child who does nothing but ape his father's opinions has, like the Jews of Isaiah's day, a faith which is *a commandment of men learned by rote* (Isa 29.13), rather than learned by personal study, meditation, and conviction.

Both of my sons have slightly differing views from mine about some passages of scripture. I'm glad. It means they have taken root on their own and, though there is never any guarantee, I feel much more optimistic about their remaining faithful when I am gone. If you remember the story of the orange tree my mother-in-law gave us, which rooted itself while we were trying to find a place to put it, here is yet another application: children need to have a little freedom in their quest for spirituality, freedom to spread their own roots. Parents who demand exact conformity, treating any difference as a sign of disrespect, are spoon-feeding their children's spirituality while at the same time stunting their growth. They might as well be carrying them off the ground in a black plastic nursery pot so their roots won't branch out. Sooner or later they will become pot-bound and die.

While you expect to shape their values and instill basic concepts of spirituality and faith, God expected that they would ask, "Why?" and that you would give them real and sensible answers. "Because I said so," does have an appropriate time and place in teaching them authority, but not in teaching the word of God. If you cannot tell them why, then when you are gone why should they continue?

Encourage them to study and develop on their own. Treat their discoveries as equally interesting as yours. You may think Paul wrote Hebrews and they may not. You may believe the three-person interpretation of the Song of Solomon and they may prefer the two-person. You may look at Romans 7 as any man without Christ, while they believe Paul is talking about himself before his conversion. Isn't it great? You will most likely have an eternity to discuss these things together and with the authors themselves, while the parents who demanded absolute conformity and automaton feedback, may find themselves looking around, wondering where their children are.

> *And the people came up out of the Jordan on the tenth day of the first month, and encamped in Gilgal, on the east border of Jericho. And those twelve stones, which they took out of the Jordan, did Joshua set up in Gilgal. And he spoke unto the children of Israel, saying, When your children shall ask their fathers in time to come, saying, What mean these stones? Then you shall let your children know, saying, Israel came over this Jordan on dry land. For Jehovah your God dried up the waters of the Jordan from before you, until you were passed over, as Jehovah your God did to the Red Sea, which he dried up from before us, until we were passed over; that all the peoples of the earth may know the hand of Jehovah, that it is mighty; that you may fear Jehovah your God for ever.*
>
> Joshua 4.19–24

19. A Hum in the Blueberries

The blueberries are in full bloom, more blooms than we have had in several years. Evidently, a long, cold winter helps production.

I walked past them the other morning, the eastern sun shining straight into those white blossoms and nearly blinding me, when I thought I heard something. I stopped and listened. Sure enough, there was a hum coming from the blueberries. Even with all the birdsong going on around me, the dogs yipping and playing in the field, and the truck traffic on the highway through the woods, that hum was loud and clear. It was nearly as loud as the fan motor in our air conditioner.

I couldn't see them, but a sudden whining zipping past my face told me the answer to my unspoken question—bees. The bushes were full of them.

A preacher's wife I know once told me about a congregation she had worshipped with for awhile. She had run into someone in the community who did not have any reticence about telling her what he thought about that group—those people would never do anything for anyone, not even each other. They were known for going to church on Sunday and then ignoring everyone else the rest of the week, including their own brethren.

You cannot read the New Testament without having your nose rubbed in the fact that the early Christians were indeed known by their communities, but for exactly the opposite sorts of things. They were in each other's homes constantly. They were helping others at every opportunity that arose, both believers and outsiders. Paul told the women who had been widowed young that they should remarry so they could stay busy; he told the older men that they should be an example of good deeds to the younger. Peter told Christians that their good deeds would "put to silence the ignorance of foolish men."

There should be a hum about the church, a busy hive of activity, showing the character of Christ through, not only our "incorrupt doctrine and sound speech," but the good we do for others. What exactly did Christ say to those goats in the Matthew 25 judgment scene parable? They were lost because they did not do for others, because by not doing for others they had not done for their Lord either.

It is a shame that somewhere a church that claims to be a part of the Lord's body is known for doing absolutely nothing. "They profess that they know God, but by their works they deny him, being abominable and disobedient and unto every good work reprobate" (Titus 1.16).

Wherever you are today, make sure you are not the one in question. Keep the hum alive.

> *Looking for the blessed hope and appearing of the glory of the great God and our Savior Jesus Christ, who gave himself for us that he might redeem us from all iniquity and purify until himself a people for his own possession, zealous of good works.*
>
> Titus 2.13–14

20. Cutworms

Cutworms are ugly, fat, brown worms that can wreak havoc overnight in a garden. They rise to the surface, wrap themselves around the tender stems of new plants, and cut them off at ground level. In the morning you find plant after plant, cut off and lying on the ground, shriveling in the new dawn.

Gardeners espouse various cures for cutworms. Some place plastic or foil collars around the stems from just above ground level to several inches below. Others insert nails, Popsicle sticks or toothpicks in the ground, one on either side of each stem. We generally just pick up a pile of twigs from the yard and poke them down next to the stems. All these cures work because they keep the worms from being able to surround the stem and cut it down. At least with our way, you don't have to walk the garden removing things that either won't degrade or might be dangerous. Just ask my son Nathan about toothpicks and bare feet.

These cures work for souls as well. People who face the trials and cares of life alone, without any support or encouragement, might as well have Satan wrap them up in his arms. They are that vulnerable. As vigilant soldiers of Christ we should be on the lookout during times when we find ourselves alone. Are you the only one at school who even claims to be a Christian? The only one at work? The only one in your neighborhood? Make sure you are not too proud to recognize moments of weakness and ask someone for help. Be willing to seek companionship when you need it. In fact, be willing to *run* for it!

And to those who are never alone, who are blessed enough to have a Christian mate or to work in a Christian atmosphere, pay attention to those around you who are not. Find the singles, the widows, the ones who have been left by unfaithful spouses, and be the someone who stands next to her so the devil cannot wrap her up and cut her down. We are too often so involved in our own families that we do not look for or make time for the lonely souls who need us. They are always the "fifth wheel," not a couple, and so they are ignored because they don't fit in. *It is our job to fit them in.*

Look around you today and find a loner. Don't let anyone lose his soul because you didn't even think to wrap him up in your encouraging arms and let him know that he is not alone.

> *Two are better than one, because they have a good reward for their toil. For if they fall, one will lift up his fellow. But woe to him who is alone when he falls and has not another to lift him up! Again, if two lie together, they keep warm, but how can one keep warm alone? And though a man might prevail against one who is alone, two will withstand him—a threefold cord is not quickly broken.*
>
> Ecclesiastes 4.9–12

21. Azaleas

When we first moved here, nearly 28 years ago, I knew I wanted azaleas around the house. And I wanted as many different colors as possible—none of this all white or all purple or all pink business. We planted about two dozen and once they started blooming, I discovered why some people stick with one type and color—they all bloom at once that way. You don't have spots of color here and there, with blank, green places in the middle of the row. So I have learned to live with those spaces, and to accept that some will bloom before others—first the white and the coral pink, followed by the lilac and pale pink, then the red and purple, and finally the bubble gum pinks, the two that frame the front door. I was a little disappointed at first, but it no longer bothers me. This is just the way it is when you have different varieties of azalea.

That's the way it is when you have different people in the body of Christ as well. None of us are at exactly the same stages in our growth. Sometimes it is because we are just starting and have little or no background in the scriptures. Sometimes it is because we have brought a lot of mistaken beliefs to the table that we have to overcome. And some of us are just a little slower than others to grasp new ideas, either from lack of comprehension or cautious skepticism.

God never expected us all to be in the same place at the same time. He spent quite a few chapters in the New Testament epistles telling us to respect one another regardless. Jesus told a whole parable about accepting the late-comers without resentment. After all, who is accepted is God's business not ours.

Some of us seem to have a problem with this. I have heard far too many comments about "them" lately, referring to the ones we see as holding us back. It usually comes in a tone of disdain, while making of ourselves some elite spiritually mature group that ought to be looked up to and heeded automatically. After all, look how much more knowledgeable we are. The epistles talk a lot about that attitude too. "Love is *patient and kind;* love does not envy or boast; *it is not arrogant*" (1 Cor 13.4), comes quickly to mind. We all know the word "longsuffering," but we seem to ignore the "long" and home in on the "suffering," which we don't think we have to do for "them." After all, "they" are holding back the progress of the gospel.

Truth to be told, when stubborn self-will enters the picture, that may be the case. In that instance, the wisdom of the elders decides when it is time to move on, even if some get left behind—or in fact, leave. That is why we have those men—to be strong enough to make those unpopular decisions and wise enough to know when to.

Far more often, God expects us to "wait for one another" in all its various applications. He expects us not to "set at nought" the one who just can't quite get it yet. Check your other translations of Romans 14.3. That phrase means to despise, to disrespect, to count as nothing. It means we think his opinion is worthless. The words may not have been used, but the contempt in them says exactly the same thing.

God would certainly expect better of those who are supposedly so much more advanced. Of all people, they should be tolerant with the many varieties of azalea among us. We all bloom in our own time. We are all beautiful to God, if not to each other. As long as everyone is striving to grow and serve the Lord to the best of their abilities, we are all equal in God's eyes, and certainly should be to one another.

> *Who are you to pass judgment on the servant of another? It is before his own master that he stands or falls. And he will be*

upheld, for the Lord is able to make him stand...Why do you pass judgment on your brother? Or you, why do you despise your brother? For we will all stand before the judgment seat of God; for it is written, "As I live, says the Lord, every knee shall bow to me, and every tongue shall confess to God." So then each of us will give an account of himself to God.

Romans 14.4, 10–12

22. The Real McCoy

I was watching the sprinkler zzzt-zzzt-zzzt its way across the garden the other day. Usually the end of April and most of May are dry. The afternoon thundershowers don't start until the humidity and temperature both reach the 90s, so to keep the garden alive, we have to irrigate. Keith has various methods he uses, a drip hose, a sprinkler, and simple hand-watering, depending upon the crop and its weaknesses. Some plants are more prone to fungus, so you keep their leaves as dry as possible by hand-watering, directing the water to the bottom of the plant. Sometimes Keith spends as long as two hours in an evening watering.

But as soon as the summer rains start, the garden takes off. It becomes obvious that, despite all the time spent, all we did was help the garden survive until the real thing came along. The plants almost explode they grow so much faster and produce so much better. Chemically the water may be the same, but out here in the country everyone knows that irrigation is a distant second to God's watering.

Should that surprise us? Adam and Eve made themselves aprons of fig leaves. God came along and made them garments of skins. I know which one I had rather wear on a cool evening. Men made gods of stone and wood and metal. Jehovah is a spirit with no beginning or end. I know which one I had rather rely on to take care of me. Under the old covenant, the blood of bulls and goats could only put away the sins for a year at a time. The blood of a perfect, unblemished sacrifice puts them away forever. I know which one I had rather count on for my salvation.

When it comes to God, there is no substitute for the real thing.

> *God understands the way to it, and he knows its place. For he looks to the ends of the earth and sees everything under the heavens. When he gave to the wind its weight, and apportioned the waters by measure, when he made a decree for the rain and a way for the lightning of the thunder, then he saw it and declared it, he established it and searched it out. And he said to man, Behold, the fear of the Lord, that is wisdom, and to turn away from evil is understanding.*
>
> Job 28.23–28

23. The Blown-Over Jasmine

My jasmine vine had a super-trellis built by a man who believes that if a little is good, more is better.

The trellis itself is a lattice of thick metal wires called a "cow panel," used for the gate portion of pasture fence. A cow isn't even going to bend it, much less push through it. The panel was stood on end and woven through a piece of twenty foot antenna mast set five feet deep into the ground. The fifteen feet above ground was held steady by nylon cord tied to two nearby trees.

The jasmine had already been growing five years, twisting its way up the fifteen feet of lattice work, and hanging over the top at least four feet. Most of the blooms were bunched near the top every year, the sides down toward the bottom thinner in both leaf and blossom. Still that huge vine was a beauty every spring and its scent often wafted on the breeze a good fifty feet away.

Then last summer, after the spring blooms had been spent, an afternoon thunderstorm blew through. Winds gusting up to forty miles an hour bore down on our property, littering the yard with limbs and twigs, moss and air plants. Afterward, we walked the place mentally adding up the hours of clean-up in our future. Then we headed down the drive and when we passed the two azaleas and two young oaks announcing the beginning of our yard, we saw the jasmine.

The two cords had snapped from the tension the winds had put on them and then the mast had simply bent over in a salaam toward the wood pile. It wasn't broken or even creased, just bowed in an arc. The weight of that vine simply couldn't stand on its own against the gusts. The "top" of the trellis now hung only a foot or so off the ground. Keith got beneath it and tried to stand it up, but the weight was too much for him alone. It would take at least two men pushing, while a truck pulled with a rope.

A few days later, before we had had a chance to do anything about it, we walked out again and discovered new growth all over the "side" of the jasmine vine, the side that was now the "top." It looked like the vine would not only survive, but thrive. So we found a section of eight inch PVC pipe that would stand on its end six feet high, and used it to prop the end of the bent trellis.

Within a few weeks the shoots on the vine were thickening all over the new top, and dangling off the sides. It was obvious we would no longer have a fifteen foot tall sentinel welcoming guests, but a fifteen foot long hedge four feet high would do just as nicely.

This past spring white blossoms covered the entire length of it, not just the mass at the end that used to be the top. The white was almost solid because the blooms were so thick and on some mornings you could smell it all the way across the field.

We don't realize it, but the times when the storms of life hit us, are often the times our faith and strength shows best. When a trellis stands on its own on a calm day, so what if the vine blooms? Would we expect otherwise? But when the storm comes and the trellis is damaged, yet it not only continues to support the vine the best it can, but the blooms actually increase, now that's worth noticing.

When life is easy, of course we can stay faithful. Isn't that what Satan said about Job? But when a trial comes along, how we handle it can be a far more powerful witness of Christ in us than any service we might have given, any class we might have taught, any check we might have offered. Just like that bent over jasmine, our blooms will show brighter and influence more people when we faithfully endure the worst Satan flings at us.

Are you dealing with a storm in your life? Don't think your usefulness to God and his people is finished. Don't think that because some servant of Satan blew you over that you have lost your value. How you handle it, the fact that you keep on standing for the Lord, even if a little bent, will be seen by many more than ever before. The blooms will be so thick, and the scent so heady, that your example will not be missed. You may think you are of no more benefit to God, but He says otherwise. Those who appreciate you will stand under your bower and give you support, but the work you are doing as you persevere is still a service far more precious than you could ever have imagined.

> *But the path of the righteous is like the light of dawn, which shines brighter and brighter until full day.*
>
> Proverbs 4.18

24. Stinkbugs

While I have kept three or four potted herbs on my steps for several years, it has only been a short while that I have grown an herb garden—two kinds of parsley, three kinds of basil, plus thyme, oregano, marjoram, dill, sage, cilantro, rosemary, mint, and chives.

I'm still learning some things the hard way. Dill must be planted in late fall because it cannot tolerate the heat of a Florida summer. Basil will stop growing when the weather cools, whether you protect it from the frost or not. Oregano is a ground runner and needs a lot of room. You must snip your chives from the bottom—not just trim off the tops—if you expect them to replenish. One recipe for pesto will decimate a basil plant for at least two weeks. Always give mint its own separate bed, or better still, pot, because it will take over the joint if you don't.

And, Keith hates cilantro. Although I am not exactly sure how he knows this, he says it tastes "like stinkbugs." We discovered this when I sprinkled chopped fresh cilantro over a turkey tortilla casserole. Now cilantro does have a distinctive flavor. While it bears a close physical resemblance to Italian flat-leaf parsley, the strongest flavored parsley, its flavor is probably ten times stronger than that herb. There IS such a thing as too much cilantro. On the other hand, a lot of people like it in moderation, including me. I guess there is no accounting for tastes.

And that is why some people reject Jesus. To some people life tastes sweeter when we do things His way. The difficult times become easier to bear, and the good times more than we dared hope for. But other people see in Him a restrictive cage denying them all the pleasures of life. Their focus on the here and now keeps them from seeing the victory of Eternity, but even worse, they are blinded by Satan to the true joys a child of God can have in this life as well. "...And exercise yourself unto godliness; for bodily exercise is profitable for a little, but godliness is profitable for all things, *having the promise of the life that now is,* and of that which is to come" (1 Tim 4.7–8). We can have joy, peace, hope, love, and fellowship with both God and the best people on earth, *while* on this earth.

But they just can't see it. I guess to them, godliness tastes like stinkbugs. Truly, there is just no accounting for tastes.

> *For we are a sweet smell of Christ unto God, in them that are saved, and in them that perish; to the one a smell from death unto death, and to the other a smell from life unto life.*
>
> 2 Corinthians 2.15–16

25. Weeds

It has become more difficult each year to find the varieties of tomato and pepper plants we want for our garden. So we invested in some grow lights and have grown 80–90 percent from seed since then.

When it comes time to transplant them into the garden, they must first become inured to the outdoors. We set them out in the sunlight, which in this subtropical clime is more direct than the rest of the country, for an hour the first time, and then move them to the shade. Every day they get more sunlight until they are ready for full sun all day.

Despite all this care, we lose a few each year. One morning, as I was putting out the last of the pepper plants, I reflected on how tenacious the weeds were. If I had been transplanting them, I wouldn't have had to worry. Even weeds half an inch tall had a root system five times their length and never wilted in the sun, while the foot high vegetables not only wilted, but often fell over. In fact, this year we simply threw away half a dozen plants because it was obvious they would never stand up to the rigors of garden growth. They were prima donnas, requiring high maintenance to simply stay alive. I doubt they would have ever produced fruit so they were not worth the trouble.

As we grow spiritually, I fear too many of us have become *prima donna* plants. When I see parents treating their girls like princesses, giving in to their every wish and making sure that life is always exciting and fun, I cringe to think what their poor husbands will be going through to keep them happy, and wonder how they will ever be able to stand by him in a crisis—they will simply fall apart. In all areas, growing up is about becoming stronger, not about gaining more privileges.

God expects the same from his children. We are supposed to become stronger, able to withstand a spiritual beating without losing our faith, willing even to face persecution for the sake of the gospel. God does shelter us when we are young in the faith, promising never to give us more than we can handle, but I think some of us are trying to hang on to our spiritual immaturity, thinking that as long as we cannot handle a trial, God will never send one! I am afraid it doesn't work that way.

God has always had a schedule for his people. He says that we should be able to teach "by reason of time." He has always pictured his people in agricultural terms, vineyards and olive-yards especially, and everyone knows that the harvest comes on a schedule—you can't put it off. "The field is white unto harvest," he told his apostles. He often seemed to despair when they hadn't grown quite fast enough to suit him: "Have I been with you so long and still you do not know me?" Just as we expect our children to become strong enough to handle life by the time they are grown, God expects the same from us. It is simply wrong to expect him to pamper us forever.

When God despairs of a people ever being able to stay faithful, he uproots them and plants something else. It may look like a weed to us. I am sure the Jews thought that God would never settle for a Gentile, but he most certainly did. And he will dig us up and toss us out for someone we might never have given the time of day if we don't develop a good enough root system to withstand the scorching heat of life's noonday sun and the floods of a spiritual downpour. He will simply look out into the field and find a weed that can take it, that doesn't have to be treated like a hothouse flower to survive. Weeds, you see, are simply uncultivated flowers—*wild*flowers—and he can make them into the beautiful plant he wants, the one that can stand the weather and stay faithful.

But if some of the branches were broken off, and you, although a wild olive shoot, were grafted in among the others and now share in the nourishing root of the olive tree, do not be arrogant toward the branches. If you are, remember it is not you who support the root, but the root that supports you. Then you will say, "Branches were broken off so that I might be grafted in." That is true. They were broken off because of their unbelief, but you stand fast through faith. So do not become proud, but fear. For if God did not spare the natural branches, neither will he spare you.

Romans 11.17–21

26. A Six Inch Pot of Mums

Several years ago I received a pot of rust colored chrysanthemums as a gift. I enjoyed them for many days before they began to fade.

"Well that's that," I thought as I placed them on the outside workbench so Keith could salvage the dark green plastic pot for other uses. By the time he got to them, they were brown and withered, as dead looking as any plant I had ever seen.

Keith cannot stand to throw things away. "It might come in handy," he always says as he pulls things out of the trash. That is why he stuck those dried out flowers in the ground beneath the dining room window. Yet even he was amazed when a few days later green leaves sprouted on those black stems. It was fall, a mum's favorite season, and before long I had twice as many as I had started with.

Fast forward to Thanksgiving, a year later. I now had a bed full of rust colored mums about two feet square. The next year the bed was four feet wide and my amaryllises were swamped. Keith built a raised bed about eight feet square, half of it for the mums and the rest for a plumbago, a miniature rose, and a blue sage. That has lasted exactly one year. The plumbago, rose, and sage have been evicted by the mums and need a new home.

What started as one six inch pot of mums, withered and brown, has become 64 square feet of blooms so thick they sprawl over the timbers of the raised bed into the field surrounding it. Whenever I cut an armful for a vase inside, you cannot even tell where I cut them.

We often fall prey to the defeatist attitude, "What can one person do?" Much to the delight of our Adversary we sit alone in the nursery pot, wither, and die. Yet the influence we have as Christians can spread through our families, our workplaces, our neighborhoods, and our communities. The good deeds we do, the moral character we show, the words we do—and don't—say make an impression on others. Those are the seeds we plant, never giving in to the notion that one person cannot accomplish anything. The attitudes we show when mistreated and the peace with which we face life's trials will make others ask, "Why? Can I have this too? How?"

Plant a seed every chance you get. If a six inch pot of dried up mums can spread so quickly, just think what the living Word of God shown through your life can accomplish.

> *And he said, How shall we liken the kingdom of God? Or in what parable shall we set it forth? It is like a grain of mustard seed, which, when it is sown upon the earth, though it be less than all the seeds that are upon the earth, yet when it is sown, grows up, and becomes greater than all the herbs, and puts out great branches, so that the birds of the heaven can lodge under the shadow thereof.*
>
> Mark 4.30–32

27. Blueberry Season

Every other morning in June I stepped outside into the morning steam of dew rising off the grass, head and eyes shielded from the bright sunshine, and carried a five quart plastic bucket to our small stand of a dozen blueberry bushes. It always amazes me how the morning temperature can be twenty degrees cooler than the afternoon's, yet within minutes the perspiration is rolling from hairline to chin. Even the dogs refuse to accompany me, though a shade tree stands within mere feet of the blueberries. They sit on the carport, their bellies flat against the still cool cement and watch, probably commenting to one another about how silly humans can be.

It was so uncomfortable one morning, and the blueberries so plenteous, their weight bending the boughs in deep arcs, that after the first half hour I became a little less careful in my picking. Often as I reached deep into the interior of a bush where I had seen several plump, ripe, dusky blueberries hanging, I simply wrapped my hand around the clump and gently nudged each one with my thumb. Berries that are ready to be picked will fall off the stem easily, and usually I pulled out a fistful of perfectly ripe ones. Once in awhile though, a red one appeared in my palm, and even a white or green one. Oh well, it certainly speeded up the process to pick that way, then toss out the bad ones, and it's not like we had a measly crop this year.

I wonder sometimes if we aren't too careful in our attempts to reach the lost. We have a bad habit of deciding who will listen before we ever start talking and our judgments are so different that the ones the Lord made. He cast his nets into a polluted river, hoping to save as many dying fish as possible; we cast ours into the country club swimming pool, but that is another metaphor for another time.

Sometimes we come across a blueberry bush with most of the berries still red, not quite ripe for the picking so we pass it by and leave a couple of big ripe ones, just begging to be put into the pie. It is too much trouble to go after them one at a time.

Other times we see a bush with quite a few plump ripe berries and instead of just reaching out and grabbing all we can, because there are a few not quite ready, we move to another branch. No need picking a handful when we might need to throw out half of them. And so we only reach for the easy ones, the ones that appeal to us because they look like the pictures in the cookbook and are easy to get to. Those showing a hint of red at the stem end might take a little more effort, a little more sugar in the pie filling. And because of that we miss some that would give our pie more flavor.

In another figure Jesus told us to sow the seed wherever we could, not take the time to map it into suitable planting zones. He said the world is ripe for picking. "Don't cast your pearls before swine," is about people who have had their chance and rejected it, not about us judging another's suitability to be our brethren. Where would we have wound up if people had treated us that way?

Go pick some blueberries. Grab all you can and let the Lord decide which ones will make the best pie.

> *But when he saw the multitudes he was moved with compassion for them because they were distressed and scattered, as sheep not having a shepherd. Then he said to his disciples, the harvest indeed is plenteous, but the laborers are few. Pray therefore the Lord of the harvest that he send forth laborers into his harvest.*
>
> Matthew 9.36–38

28. Transplants

We recently discovered a new wildflower, a fifteen foot long vine with delicate, featherlike leaves, and bright red tubular blooms with a star-shaped flare. Keith brought some home from the woods and stuck them in several plastic nursery pots. Now, several weeks later, they are doing just fine. When I looked them up and found their name, Cypress Vine, I also discovered that they are often sold as garden annuals under the name Red Morning Glory, but that they proved so hardy they have spread to the wild, including the wild just across my fence.

Hardy indeed when all you have to do is take a cutting, stick it in the dirt, and water it until it roots. Not every plant is so easy. Sometimes you must root them in water. Sometimes you must get a product like Rootone, dipping the ends of the cutting into that powder before you try to root it. But all transplants have this in common—they deserve special care. Transplant shock can claim even the strongest of specimens without it.

The same is true when we convert a sinner to the gospel. Transplanting him from a world of sin to the rarefied air of the redeemed can be more than his system can handle. So he needs special care. Too many times I have seen churches baptize a man then say, "Whew! Now he's okay," and leave him standing in the midst of surroundings so alien to him that he withers and dies almost immediately. It may not seem alien to us, but we are used to it. We took root many years ago and now we stand strong and able to endure temptations, trials, and even the mere tedium of life. Why do we expect a cutting from the world to instantly take root and blossom? We treat our garden flowers far better than our new brethren.

Even a cutting described as "hardy" needs daily attention. I expect my Cypress vines to bloom vigorously this time next year. But I don't expect them to suddenly grow to their usual fifteen feet covered with flaming red flowers before then. Why are we so impatient with our new brothers and sisters in the Lord? It is worth it to take the time with them, nurturing their growth as we would our own gardens, so that we can bask in their beauty just a little while down the road.

Agriculture is hard work. Jesus talked about *laborers* in his vineyard, not people simply strolling through, taking the tour so they could have a free wine tasting at the end. You don't get to taste his wine when you don't work to care for his grapes.

> *Strengthen the weak hands, and make firm the feeble knees. Say to those who have an anxious heart, "Be strong; fear not! Behold, your God will come with vengeance, with the recompense of God. He will come and save you."*
>
> Isaiah 35.3–4

29. Ladybugs

Gardeners know about ladybugs. These tiny beetles can eat up to 50,000 aphids *each* in their two to three year lifespan. That isn't all they eat. Leaf hoppers and mites and even some types of plant mildew make a meal for them. You can buy a supply of ladybugs if you want. I forget the exact numbers, but you can get several thousand for about $25. Or you could let a bunch of dandelions grow up between the rows of your vegetables. Evidently those attract ladybugs, but dandelions in the garden? I don't think so.

We have never had many ladybugs that I have noticed. A few days ago though, as I bent to weed the okra yet again, I suddenly noticed on the leaf right under my nose an oval orange bug with black spots on it. A ladybug! I looked them up afterward, and I think the most interesting discovery was how they fend off their predators. They give off a stinky secretion from their joints. They are the skunks of the insect world.

Several times in the Old Testament you see the phrase, "They became a stench in the nostrils. . . ." More than once God's people began to stink up the place, either to the enemy they defeated by the hand of God, or to God himself when they began to live like their enemies.

The same thing can happen to us. I remember when we lived in town and occasionally had one of those knocks on the door. Usually those folks never came back—not because we were rude, but because we obviously knew the word of God and were not afraid to answer the questions they pose to get your interest. I think the fact that we had an answer to begin with threw them off track. One time we saw the same people come down our street a few weeks later. When they got to our property line, they actually crossed the street so they wouldn't be walking any closer to us than they had to, then crossed back to get to our next door neighbors. I guess we had begun to smell.

Funny how the same thing can smell good to one and not the other. Paul said, "For we are the aroma of Christ to God among those who are being saved and among those who are perishing, to one a fragrance from death to death, to the other a fragrance from life to life" (2 Cor 2.15–16). When Paul and his entourage preached, some people liked it and some didn't. When we live the word of God in front of people, especially when we speak it, the same thing will happen to us.

Maybe that makes us ladybugs, saving the world from the pests with the sword of the spirit, the word of God, and saving ourselves the same way—repelling our foes with a smell they simply cannot stand—the sweet aroma of redemption. Isn't that a good enough reason to get out your vial of God's perfume this morning, and become a little more familiar with it? God is counting on us ladybugs.

> *But thanks be to God, who in Christ always leads us in triumphal procession, and through us spreads the fragrance of the knowledge of him everywhere.*
>
> 2 Corinthians 2.14

30. How Does Your Garden Grow?

In drought times, not very well. I remember a particular summer not too long ago. The ground was powder dry. Even my dog raised a dust cloud chasing a tennis ball. In three months we had only six-tenths of an inch of rain. Dew hadn't even fallen.

Ordinarily, we plant our garden in mid-March, and it is well up and growing by the end of the month. That year we followed the usual pattern, and by April 1 we were replanting—nothing came up in many rows and the rest were sparse. If you are a gardener, you know that squash is the easiest thing in the world to grow. You can practically throw it at the ground and within a month you can supply a city the size of New York. After two weeks we didn't even have one half inch seedling in the whole row!

So water it, you say? We did. Faithfully. Every evening. Still nothing.

When we decided to replant, we went down the same rows, planting the same things. When we dug new rows, there lay the old seed, looking just like it did when it came out of the package, no germination at all. You know what we discovered? The watering job we did was not deep enough to reach the seeds, in spite of the fact that we spent two hours at it every night.

So we replanted, this time watering the row *before* we covered it, and watering much longer every night afterward. The seeds came shoving their way up through the dirt before a week was out, and some of the old ones sprouted too. It wasn't long till people went running when they saw us approaching with our buckets of squash.

Even after 32 years of gardening we learned something. Growth happens with deep watering, not shallow. And it takes an effort to get it as deeply as you should. It's not something you can do with a half-hearted, rushed effort. We're so used to "labor-saving devices" that I wonder if we even recognize real work, because that's what it takes.

God's people in the Old Testament had a watering problem as well. They thought that serving God was simply a matter of following prescribed rituals. Despite daily reciting a passage from the Torah that began "Thou shalt love the Lord thy God with all they heart," they never got within an inch of their hearts. They "celebrated" the Sabbath, all the time watching the clock, hoping it would be over with soon. They offered sacrifices, the lame and blind, and anything else that didn't cost them too much. They fasted, a ritual they called "afflicting the soul," which never once touched their souls.

Now, how is *my* spiritual garden growing? Maybe I need to do some deep watering.

> *Is this the fast I have chosen? The day for a man to afflict his soul? Is it to bow down his head in a rush and to spread sackcloth and ashes under him? Will you call this a fast and an acceptable day to Jehovah? Is not* ***this*** *the fast that I have chosen: to loose the bonds of wickedness, to undo the bands of the yoke, and to let the oppressed go free, and that you break every yoke? Is it not to deal your bread to the hungry, and that you bring the poor that are cast out to your house? When you see the naked that you cover him, and that you hide not yourself from your own flesh and blood?...If you take away from the midst of you the yoke, the pointing finger, and the malicious talk, and if you draw out your soul to the hungry and satisfy the afflicted soul, then shall light rise in darkness, and your obscurity be as noonday. And Jehovah*

will guide you continually, and satisfy your soul in the dry places, and make strong your bones and you shall be like a watered garden, and like a spring of water, whose waters fail not.

Isaiah 58.5–11

31. Dehydration

That garden of ours is a lot of work. In Florida that means it is also a lot of sweat. When Keith comes in from a summertime Saturday of hoeing, weeding, mulching, spraying, mowing, and picking, he must leave his work clothes hanging on the porch because the hems are literally dripping.

Losing that much fluid can be dangerous. Dehydration can cause nausea, vomiting, muscle cramps, lightheadedness, and heart palpitations as the body tries to pump the same amount of blood with less liquid to accomplish the task. If the body is not re-hydrated, confusion will follow, and eventually coma, organ failure, and death.

It is important to keep your body hydrated as you go along and not wait until you are thirsty. Keith always carries a gallon jug of water out with him to set in the shade of the carport while he works. Every time he has a break in the activity—a finished row, an accomplished chore, an errand that takes him past the carport—he stops to take a drink even if he doesn't think he needs it. If you wait until you are thirsty, dehydration has already set in.

I like to think of our Sunday assemblies as our chance to rehydrate. Nothing can sap your energy and drain your spiritual reservoirs like a week out in the world. Without replenishing ourselves on a regular basis, we can suffer spiritual dehydration. Trials become harder to bear and temptations more difficult to overcome. The carnal, selfish attitudes that surround us can drain our faith. Suddenly we hit a critical point, a time when our souls wrest in a spiritual cramp, and if we do not top up the tanks, a spiritual heat stroke in on the horizon. If we wait too long, coma—an indifference to our situation—and spiritual death will soon follow.

When the assembly of the saints works as it was intended, it reminds us that we are not alone, encourages us with the hope of the gospel, strengthens the muscles that have grown weak with exhaustion, and replenishes the faith, "provoking one another to love and good works." That meeting that we so often do nothing but complain about is as essential to our spiritual health as water is to our bodies.

But you can't just sit there looking at the water bottle and expect to gather strength from it. You can't expect someone to hold it for you. Your mama quit doing that a long time ago. Rehydration takes at least enough effort to pick up the bottle, lift it to your lips, and swallow.

You don't need it every week, you say? Yes, you do. If you wait till you're thirsty, damage has already been done to your soul. If you know what's good for you, you'll take a sip every chance you get.

> *Jesus said to her, "Everyone who drinks of this water will be thirsty again, but whoever drinks of the water that I will give him will never be thirsty again. The water that I will give him will become in him a spring of water welling up to eternal life."*
>
> John 4.13–14

32. Erect Rosemary

A couple of years ago when I went to a local garden shop to buy another rosemary plant, I learned something more about these herbs I have grown so fond of.

"Which kind would you like?" the woman said, "prostrate or erect?"

That was the first I had ever heard of two types of rosemary. Finally I knew why the rosemary plants in my favorite TV cook's garden stood so straight, while mine just splayed out like they were tired all the time. I bought an erect rosemary, the first I had ever had, and you can certainly tell the difference as the two plants bed side by side.

After only a little contemplation I realized those are exactly the same two types of people—those who try to stand on their own, unwilling to yield to the will of God, and those who prostrate themselves before him in an attitude of worshipful submission.

We seldom actually fall prostrate before God these days. The closest I remember seeing this was when I was a small child and some of the men knelt or sat back on their haunches in the aisles, one knee up to hold an elbow during public prayers at church, something I even remember my Daddy doing. Most of us are too self-conscious to do that sort of thing now. If someone tried it he might be accused of "praying for show." I've heard similar things in the not too distant past as we so Pharisaically try to rid ourselves of Phariseeism.

Surely, though, we have all reached a point of despair in our lives when we simply throw ourselves on the bed or the floor and lay ourselves and our problems before God. While it certainly isn't the outward posture that makes the prayer acceptable to God, one can't help wondering if a *refusal* to ever "fall prostrate" doesn't expose a heart that will not fall prostrate either.

One of the definitions of "worship" is exactly that: to fall prostrate before. We are not truly worshiping if our hearts do not recognize the absolute sovereignty of God and our utter dependence upon him for both physical and spiritual survival. That dependence, that prostrate attitude, must be accompanied by instant and total obedience. Too many today think they can "worship" on Sundays with weekday lifestyles that never come close to the one Jesus expected of his followers. When our choices follow the choices of the world, it is the Prince of the World we are falling prostrate before, not God.

This morning I stretched out the limbs of my prostrate rosemary to their full length and they actually reached higher than the erect one. Isn't that true of a person who prostrates himself before God? "Therefore I will boast all the more gladly of my weaknesses that the power of Christ may rest upon me…for when I am weak, then I am strong (2 Cor 12.9–10).

So think today about the two types of rosemary. Which one are you? The one who insists on reaching for the stars on his own, or the one who depends upon the Creator of those stars to help him reach his full potential, trusting and obeying implicitly? Even the erect rosemarys will some day fall on their faces before the King of all: "As I live, says the Lord, to me every knee shall bow, and every tongue shall confess to God" (Rom 14.11). It would be a whole lot better to do it before you are forced to.

> *And all the angels were standing around the throne and around the elders and the four living creatures, and they fell on their faces before the throne and worshiped God, saying, "Amen! Blessing and glory and wisdom and thanksgiving and honor and power and might be to our God forever and ever! Amen."*
>
> Revelation 7.11–12

33. Tending the Garden

After my herb bed gave me fits one year, Keith spent some time completely digging it out and replacing the dirt with potting soil and composted manure. That was $90 worth of dirt! That means I am spending a lot more time, and even more money, caring for it so the original costs won't be wasted.

I have gone to a real nursery to find plants, larger and more established (and more expensive) than the discount store 99 cent pots. I have dug trenches for some scalloped stone borders to help keep the encroaching lily bed out of it, and to dissuade any critters that might hide beneath the shed behind the bed from using it as a back door.

I water it every day, and fertilize it every other week. I pull out anything that somehow blows in and seeds itself in my precious black soil.

I have seedlings planted to finish the bed, varieties of herbs that are difficult to find as plants, which I had to carry in and out of the house time and time again due to the fluctuating spring temperatures. Then they were transplanted into ever-increasing sized cups as they outgrew their tiny seed sponges, before finally reaching their permanent home in the herb garden bed.

I have invested so much time, energy, and money into this herb garden that I am not about to let it die.

Why is it that we will work ourselves silly because of a monetary investment, while at the same time neglecting other things much more important to our lives?

How about your marriage? I say to every young couple I know, "Marriage is a high maintenance relationship." Right now, they think they will always be this close, always share every joy and every care. They think there will never come a time when she wonders if he still loves her, or he wonders if she cares at all about the problems he must deal with at work.

Life gets in the way. If you want to stay as close as you are during that honeymoon phase, you have to tend your little garden. Fix his favorite meal. Send her flowers. Put a love note in his lunchbox. Take out the garbage without being asked. Find a babysitter and go out on a date. Just sit down after the kids are in bed—*make* them go to bed, people—and talk to each other. *And listen!* Pray together. Study together. Worship together. Laugh together. Cry together.

What about your relationship with God? Do you think you can maintain a close relationship with someone you don't know? He gave you a whole book telling you who He is (1 Cor 2.11–13). How much time do you spend with it? How often do you talk to Him? How can He help you when you never ask? How can you enjoy being in the presence of someone with whom you have nothing in common? Disciples want nothing more than to become like their teachers (1 Pet 2.21–22; 2 Pet 3.18).

None of that comes without effort. You must spend some time and energy, maybe even make a few sacrifices to cultivate your relationship with God. When you have invested nothing, it means nothing to you, and it shows.

Spend some time today improving your marriage, tending to your family relationships, cultivating your love and care for your brethren, and most of all, caring for your soul—pulling out the weeds, feeding it, nursing it along—so it will grow into a deeper, stronger, more fruitful relationship with your God.

> *Sow to yourselves in righteousness, reap according to kindness; break up your fallow ground; for it is time to seek Jehovah, till he come and rain righteousness upon you.*
>
> Hosea 10.12

34. White Hydrangeas

When we lived in another state many years ago, we had two hydrangeas, one flanking each side of the patio steps. I loved those plants. They took little care and for that meager effort produced huge balls of blue blooms all summer. So I decided a few years ago to plant a couple here.

I understand that there are white hydrangeas that are supposed to be that way. They are often used in weddings, which seems appropriate and lovely. But most hydrangeas are not supposed to be white. Instead, the color of their blooms depends upon the pH of the soil. If there is plenty of aluminum in the soil, you get blue blooms. If aluminum is lacking, you usually get pink.

If you do not get the color you want, you can change it yourself. Mix one tablespoon of aluminum sulfate per gallon of water and use it during the growing season. (Be sure the plant is well-watered beforehand or you could burn your plants.) If you prefer pink blooms, use dolomite. I really don't care if I get pink instead of blue, but I did not want white. White is what I got.

Some people can't seem to make up their minds about serving God. They show up on Sunday morning, but you would never know it if you saw them the rest of the week. Their dress, language, recreation, and opinions match the world around them. Like God's people of old, they "fear the Lord, but serve other gods" (2 Kgs 17.33). Instead of being either pink or blue, they try to be neutral, thinking it will help them get along with both sides.

Jesus addressed their descendants in Matthew 6.24—"You cannot serve two masters," something we often try to do ourselves, giving our time and energy to the material and only the leftovers, if there are any, to the spiritual. That is why our prayers are often useless. We know we aren't pink or blue, so we pray with "doubt," like the "double-minded man, unstable in all his ways" (Jas 1.6–8).

That wasn't the end of passages I could find. "How long will you go limping between two sides?" Elijah asked (1 Kgs 18.21). "Choose this day whom you will serve," Joshua demanded (Josh 24.15). The Lord doesn't want white hydrangeas any more than I do. He wants people who can make a decision and stand by it, people who care enough to go all out, not just dabble. We cannot be wishy-washy. "If you aren't with me you are against me," Jesus told the disciples (Luke 11.23).

One of my hydrangeas has finally developed a light blue tint. Then I got my acid and alkaline colors mixed up and had Keith put hydrated lime on it. So tomorrow it may turn pink. But it really doesn't matter—one or the other, pink or blue, just not white. I didn't plant it to get some neutral color, and that isn't why God put us where He did either.

> *I know your works: you are neither cold nor hot. Would that you were either cold or hot! So, because you are lukewarm, and neither hot nor cold, I will spew you out of my mouth.*
>
> Revelation 3.15–16

35. Weeding the Lilies

My daylilies have been on a roller coaster ride lately. They bloomed so prodigiously, and multiplied so quickly that ten years ago I had to dig them up from their bed by the grape arbor and replant them thinner, planting another bed behind the shed with some of the extras, and still giving away three five-gallon bucketfuls of bulbs. They bloomed like crazy again, multiplying year by year, until once again they needed thinning.

Four years ago, Keith had to do it for me—after a summer of eye surgeries I was relegated to supervising from a lawn chair. But since then, few have come up and fewer have bloomed. Perhaps we mulched them too well, Keith thought, so he raked off half the mulch this past year to see what would happen. More blooms is what happened, and things seem better. Next year should be another banner year of bright yellow and orange blooms.

I have noticed another thing about these lilies. Even with mulch, the weeds still manage to creep in. The first year I pulled grass till my hands were sore and swollen. Blackberry thorns left them torn and bleeding, even through gloves. The next year I did it again. The third year things were better—most of the weeds were along the edge. By the fourth year two weedings, one at the beginning of the year, and another near the end, took care of it.

Some day, I would like to think that the weeding won't be necessary at all, but I live in a land of rain and sunshine, warmth even in winter, and humidity that keeps the plants green and moist. Still, it is encouraging to see some progress. I may never have a weed-free flower bed, but at least there are more flowers than weeds these days.

How about me? Am I still pulling out the weeds in my heart? Unfortunately, yes, I am. I do not believe the job will ever be finished. I do believe that there are fewer now than many years ago, and I think I am meant to notice that, that it is not a sign of arrogance to see the improvement in my life. Isn't encouragement a necessary element to growth?

That old saying, "Humility is the thing that as soon as you think you have it, you've lost it," is ridiculous. How else am I to have the impetus to keep going, especially when the job is unending and obviously so? Why is it wrong to recognize my progress? I might as well listen to Satan as to listen to someone say that.

Several times Paul told the people he wrote that they were doing well, that they had grown, that he was proud of them. James talks about looking in the mirror of God's word to see myself. Am I only supposed to see the faults and none of the good things? That is exactly what leads people to become so despondent that they quit trying.

"Might as well be hanged for a sheep as a goat," applies to people who never receive any positive feedback, who are always criticized and told they have done wrong. They think if they are going to receive that kind of response when doing their best, they might as well stop trying so hard. Satan counts on that feeling, and too often we give him the opportunity to make use of it in ourselves and others.

So look at yourself carefully today. Notice the things you still need to work on and do exactly that. But also notice where you have improved and gain some encouragement from it. Maybe the job today won't be quite so tough. If you have had a difficult time lately, that little bit of encouragement may be the thing that gets you through another day.

For you know how, like a father with his children, we exhorted each one of you and encouraged you and charged you to walk in a manner worthy of God, who calls you into his own kingdom and glory. And we also thank God constantly for this, that when you received the word of God, which you heard from us, you accepted it not as the word of men but as what it really is, the word of God, which is at work in you believers.

1 Thessalonians 2.11–13

36. Weed Killer

Keith sprayed weed killer in the plot of ground I have designated for a new flower bed. It worked just fine, weeds and grass wilting and disappearing over the next week or so until it was completely bare. We had a warm spell just before Christmas and I just noticed that a spot or two of green has erupted, even more obvious in the black ground surrounding it. What are they? Florida betony, a ground cover that spreads through a web-like array of white roots.

I think there are two lessons here—when you take out all the bad in your life, you had better fill it up with good fast or you will just have more room for evil to flourish. Jesus told his own parable about that—the house that was swept clean and the demons who moved into it (Matt 12.43–45).

But did you know this? "Weed killer" is really a misnomer. It is "plant killer." Most of those sprays cannot differentiate between one green thing and another. They don't look for dollar weed and avoid the petunias. You have to be careful with the weed killer.

Too often we are not as careful as we should be when spraying the spiritual weed killer. In our zeal to rid the world of false teaching and sin, we can do a fine job of killing the new plants too. Just as a policeman is taught to be careful of who is standing behind the fleeing criminal before he shoots, we must be careful of innocent bystanders who may be caught in the crossfire.

Knowledge carries with it great responsibility in how we use it. Too often it comes with a lack of experience and wisdom and that ice cold new term, collateral damage, becomes a frightening reality to young souls. How are we any different from the wolves when our zeal leaves bloodied and broken lambs lying around us in a heap? Many times what is passed off as zeal is simply a selfish desire to look knowledgeable and strong in the faith. Even Satan used the scriptures for his own purposes. Jesus also told a parable about leaving the weeds in the field because they had become so entangled it would have killed the wheat to pull them out (Matt 13.24–30). He had to restrain his workers who were anxious to go out and rid the world of the enemy regardless who else was hurt.

None of which is to say that even the wise will never make a mistake. Knowing when to do what can be a difficult call to make. Usually the ones who criticize, though, are the ones who sit back and do nothing when the wolves enter the flock, never placing themselves and their decisions at risk

Just think about this today: be careful with the weed killer. At times, when Keith needed to use it in spite of new plants already growing nearby, he has used shields over the tender shoots and reached in closer than usual to the weeds so that he could better control his aim.

Always be careful with the word of God. It's powerful stuff.

> *And he said unto his disciples, It is impossible but that occasions of stumbling should come; but woe unto him, through whom they come! It were well for him if a millstone were hanged about his neck, and he were thrown into the sea, rather than that he should cause one of these little ones to stumble.*
>
> Luke 17.1–2

37. The Apple Tree

My back and feet were aching and my hands cramped from peeling by the time I finished. The seals on the pint jars of apple butter popped and I started the clean-up of unused jars and lids, the large pot covered with sticky residue, and the measuring cups and spoons. Finally it was over.

The apple tree had borne far more than ever before. I had made several pies, a couple dozen muffins and a cake, and canned two dozen quarts of applesauce, a gallon of apple juice, a dozen pints of apple jelly, half a dozen quarts of apple pie filling, and finally a half dozen jars of apple butter.

As I stood over a sink full of soapy water I muttered, "I hope I never see another apple as long as I live." The next spring my apple tree died.

When it became apparent that we couldn't save the tree, Keith looked at me and muttered something about not really knowing what that might mean—the fact that I could curse a tree and it up and die for no obvious reason so soon afterward. Just exactly who, or what, was he married to?

The county agent saved my reputation. The tree was planted too close to an oak, he said. Oaks carry a disease that kills fruit trees, especially apples and peaches. Sure enough, we soon lost our peach tree too.

All these years later, the story came up again, and with it a new perspective. Here I had cursed a tree that bore too much, while the Lord cursed one that bore too little.

"And seeing in the distance a fig tree in leaf, he went to see if he could find anything on it. When he came to it, he found nothing but leaves, for it was not the season for figs. And he said to it, "May no one ever eat fruit from you again." And his disciples heard it. And as they passed by it in the morning, they saw the fig tree withered to its roots" (Mark 11.13–14, 20).

You might do as I did at first and wonder why the Lord would expect to find figs when it wasn't fig season. Yet every commentator I read said that figs produce their fruit *before* they leaf out. When the Lord saw a fig tree fully leafed out, he had every right to expect to see some fruit, even if it was small and green. As a gardener I know that nearly every plant has at least one "early-riser"—a tomato or pepper or blueberry that ripens before the others. Even if there was nothing ripe, there should have been plenty of fruit hanging there, gradually ripening on the leafy branches.

Now how about us? Is anything ripening on our branches? Is the fruit of the Spirit perhaps still a little green, but nonetheless visible as we become more and more what he would have us be? Or are we nothing but leafy show: lots of pretty clothes on Sunday morning but behavior like the rest of the world throughout the week? Lots of talk in Bible class, but no good works in the community? Quoting catchphrases to our neighbors, but never opening the Book in our own homes? More concerned with winning arguments than winning souls?

The Lord will come looking for figs in our lives, more than likely at a season in which we are not expecting him. He told us we would recognize false teachers by their fruits (Matt 7.15–20). What will he recognize about us from ours or will there even be any for him to see?

> *And so, from the day we heard, we have not ceased to pray for you, asking that you may be filled with the knowledge of his will in all spiritual wisdom and understanding, so as to walk in a manner worthy of the Lord, fully pleasing to him, bearing fruit in every good work and increasing in the knowledge of God.*
>
> Colossians 1.9–10

38. Accidental Gardeners

The garden is in full-production. We purposefully planted over a dozen different kinds of seeds and that is the only reason those particular things are growing right now. But not everything works that way. We didn't plant the grass or the dandelions or the oak trees. We didn't plant the dollar weed or the stinging nettles or the slash pines. Yet somehow, whether the wind scattering puff balls or the squirrels burying pine nuts and acorns, or the coats of furry animals grabbing onto burrs and pods as sticky as Velcro and depositing them yards or even miles from the original plants, those seeds were sown. Planting is not always on purpose. Sometimes it's accidental.

God expects us to plant the seed of the Word, recycling what was put into us. "Go therefore and make disciples of all nations," Jesus said (Matt 28.20), followed immediately by, "teaching them to observe all things I have commanded you," the first of which was to "Go make disciples." I am afraid we wait for personal evangelism systems to come our way before we even try; not realizing that we plant something every day, sometimes in spite of ourselves.

God has expected his people to teach the succeeding generations since the beginning. Noah preached for 120 years while he built that ark, and achieved nothing, right? No, he saved his family. I have known preachers who were so busy preaching and holding personal Bible studies that they completely ignored the prospects in their own homes. I have known Christians who expected the church to do their work for them, and then wondered what happened when their children fell away. "Fathers raise your children in the nurture and admonition of the Lord" (Eph 6.4), not churches, not Bible class teachers, not even mothers—FATHERS. That's where the buck stops with God.

Churches are taught to pass the gospel along. If we behave ourselves as we ought, even our mere existence "makes known the manifold wisdom of God" to the world (Eph 3.10). The teaching is internal as well. The older women are to train the younger, and the older men the younger men (Titus 2.2–8). Preachers are told to train others to preach (2 Tim 2.2). God expects his people to be farmers, planting the seed year after year, on purpose. Yet we plant accidentally too.

You plant it in your children every time they see you make an important decision. You plant it in them every time they see you study your Bible and pray. You plant it in them with home Bible studies, with family prayers, and even with your comments as you live your life. Do they see thanksgiving or griping? Do they hear love and appreciation of other Christians or backbiting and gossip?

You plant it in your friends and neighbors when they see you in the car every Sunday morning without fail. You plant it in them when they see how you handle the trials of life, or even the small nuisances. You plant it in them when you lend a hand, even unasked. You plant it in them when you say good things about your church family. You plant it in them when you invite them to a Bible study or a group service. What kinds of things do you bother to invite your friends to except the things that matter most to you?

Even when we think we aren't, we are always planting. Even fallow fields do not stay empty. Grass, weeds, and even volunteer vegetables spring up untended. "Fallow" doesn't mean bare, it means unused or idle. A fallow heart simply doesn't care what comes up. Sowing the seed is a little bit like setting an example—you do it whether you intend to or not. You are planting *something* with every word and action. Make sure it's the gospel.

Do not be deceived: God is not mocked, for whatever one sows, that will he also reap. For the one who sows to his own flesh will from the flesh reap corruption, but the one who sows to the Spirit will from the Spirit reap eternal life. And let us not grow weary of doing good, for in due season we will reap, if we do not give up.

Galatians 6.7–9

39. Rhizomes

I don't really know that much about plants. I have killed my fair share of them, especially houseplants, but I salve my ego with the notion that it might be because the house is so dark. In Florida, living under huge live oaks is good for the electric bill, not so good for anything inside that needs a sunny window.

I have learned the hard way what to do and what not to do. Living in Zone 9 means you make more mistakes than most about what will grow and what won't. It never dawned on me that there was such a thing as too warm a climate until the first time I planted tulip bulbs. All those lovely spring flowers will never make it here without a lot of extra work, like digging them up and putting them in the freezer for awhile, and even then you can't count on it.

We lived in South Carolina for three years and I could actually grow irises. The first time I ordered them, I was stunned when they arrived—a bare hunk of root in a plastic bag. Surely it was dead by now, I thought. That was how I learned about rhizomes.

Rhizomes are not ordinary roots, long and hairlike, growing out of the bottom of a stem. They aren't bulbs either. They are long pieces of thick rootstock, sometimes called underground stems, which run horizontally under the plant, sending out numerous roots and even leaf buds from its upper surface. That horizontal orientation also aids in propagation, as the roots spread underground and form more rhizomes from which more plants grow the next season.

Now think about that as you read this passage: "Therefore, as you received Christ Jesus the Lord, so walk in him, rooted and built up in him and established in the faith, just as you were taught, abounding in thanksgiving" (Col 2.6–7). That word "rooted" is the Greek word *rhizoomai*. I am not a Greek scholar but it doesn't take one to see the connection between that word and "rhizome." I am told that its figurative meaning is "to become stable."

It isn't just that we are rooted downward in the faith with tiny hairlike roots. Our faith is based in something that is strong, that can even withstand the rigors of being out of its milieu for awhile, that spreads out to others on a regular basis, and eventually grows into a whole support system. Try to pull up an ordinary plant and you can usually do so without too much trouble. Try to pull up a rhizome-based plant and you have to work at it awhile, in fact you may uproot half your yard trying to do so and still never get it all.

That sort of root takes awhile to develop. It doesn't happen overnight or without effort, and it won't happen that way with you either. You must work at it, but once you have, you will be far stronger than you ever imagined.

You have to be connected to your brethren too, you can't just "be a Christian," one completely divorced from the Lord's family, and think you will ever have that same sort of strength. Rhizomes reach out, and so must we. The only other choice is a fragile little root system that will die if it is uprooted for very long at all.

"Build up…your most holy faith," Jude says (v 20), but build it down as well, rooting yourself with a strong rootstock that will not waver, despite the trials of life and the persecutions of the enemy. Develop a rhizome and, in the words of Peter who told us how to supplement our faith, "you shall never fall" (2 Pet 1.5–10).

And you, who once were alienated and hostile in mind, doing evil deeds, he has now reconciled in his body of flesh by his death, in order to present you holy and blameless and above reproach before him, if indeed you continue in the faith, grounded and steadfast, not shifting from the hope of the gospel that you heard, which has been proclaimed in all creation under heaven.

Colossians 1.21–23

40. A Bright Spot in the Day

Shortly after this latest surgery, when I had grown weary of sitting in a dark house alone day after day, I donned a couple of pairs of sunglasses, one on top of the other, and a hat with a broad visor, picked up my walking sticks, and stepped outside. It was still morning so as long as I faced west, the light was tolerable.

The dogs heard me coming and met me at the door, bumping each other out of the way vying for the first pat, tails wagging so hard and fast they might have been declared lethal weapons. When they saw my intent to head out into the open, they took off in that direction, Magdi stiffly romping, an old dog briefly reminded of her youth, and Chloe ripping circles around her, leaving skid marks in the grass.

Right after an eye surgery, the operated-on eye sees nothing but a blur of color for a few weeks. Although the two eyes are separate entities, each with its own plumbing and wiring systems, the other eye experiences some "sympathy pains" and its vision is not as clear as usual either. While I could miss the furniture, so to speak, details were difficult. As far as I could tell there were no individual blooms on the crape myrtles—each was simply one big blotch of color. There were no leaves on the trees—they were just big puffs of green, exactly the way a child would draw them. There were no individual blades of grass—the ground was just painted green, except way out in the field where someone had spilled a bucket of yellow paint.

I headed for that spot, my two bodyguard/playmates scampering around ahead and behind, sniffing up grasshoppers the size of mascara tubes. Our ten paws were soon soaked with dew and breaded with sand. When I got close enough to see my beautiful spot of bright yellow and knelt down, it was a thick oval patch of dandelion blooms about ten feet by six feet, between the mown field and the back fence. Dandelions! I laughed out loud. My spot of beauty was what most people consider bothersome weeds. There ought to be a lesson here, I thought, and maybe this is it.

Not many of us are long stemmed red roses in God's garden, let alone rare and delicate orchids. I have met some fresh-faced petunias whose sincerity is obvious, some formal and well-dressed gladioli who can stand before a crowd and speak without fear, some pleasant and reliable carnations who seem able to function in practically any situation, and some sturdy daisies with a lot of staying power. But some of us are just dandelions, not very popular, not very talented, all too soon developing a cap of fuzzy gray hair. So do we use that as our excuse?

Do we sit back and wait for those other blooms to catch everyone's attention and take care of the business at hand? Do we still do nothing, even those times in our lives when we are the only blossom in a field full of tares and thistles? Even a dandelion looks pretty good there.

That little patch of dandelions gave me the first real laugh I'd had in weeks. It got me out of a dark, lonely house into a world of sunlight (safely at my back), and a cool breeze filled with birdsong. My soul recovered more in five minutes than my body had in the whole week before. What might my day have been like without those humble little plants?

God has a place for all of us and he won't accept excuses for doing nothing. It doesn't matter if someone else is better known, better liked, or even a whole lot more able, especially if those someones are not present when a need arises. Stop looking at yourself and look around you—self-absorption never accomplished anything.

God is the owner of this garden and He doesn't mind a dandelion or two. In fact, it seems like He made more of them than any other flower.

> *Whatever your hand finds to do, do it with your might, for there is no work nor thought nor knowledge nor wisdom in Sheol to which you are going.*
>
> Ecclesiastes 9.10

41. Picking Blackberries

For the past few years wild blackberries have been rare. The vines are there, full of their painful and aggravatingly sticky thorns, but the fruit dries up before it can fully ripen. First the drought of the late 90s, and then the following dry years of this regular weather cycle of wet and dry have meant that when the time is right, usually early to mid-June, there is nothing to pick. The few that might have survived are devoured quickly by the birds.

This year Lucas found some on a nearby service road, and Keith picked enough for one cobbler for the first time in years. Probably because it has been awhile, I think that was the best blackberry cobbler we ever had. Maybe next year I can make jelly too.

Blackberries are a lot of trouble. The thorns seem like they reach out and grab you. I have often come home with bloody hands and torn clothing—you *never* wear anything you might wear elsewhere when you pick blackberries. But that is not the half of it.

You must also spray yourself and your long-sleeved shirt prodigiously with an insect repellent, and tuck the cuffs of your long pants into your socks. No matter how hot the weather, you must be covered. Without these measures chiggers will find their way in and you will be revisiting your time in the woods far longer and in more unpleasant ways than you wish. Ticks are also a problem. Make sure you pick with someone you don't mind checking you over after you get back home, especially your hair. More than once I have had a tick crawl out of my mop of curls several hours later.

Finally, you must always carry a big stick or a pistol. I prefer pistols because you don't have to get quite as close to the snake to kill it. Birds love blackberries, and snakes like birds, so they often sit coiled under the canes waiting for their meals to fly in. Keith has killed more than one rattlesnake while picking wild blackberries.

Because of all this, since I have Keith, I seldom pick blackberries any more—I let him do it for both of us. Especially since I stand for hours in a hot kitchen afterward, it seems a fair division of labor. When I am making jelly, straining that hot juice through cheesecloth to catch the plenteous seeds and ladling that hot syrupy liquid into hot jars isn't much easier than picking them. But wild blackberries are worth all the trouble. Their scent is sweet and heady and their taste, especially in homemade jellies, almost exotic. The purple hands, teeth, and tongue blackberry lovers wind up with are worth it too. If all you have ever had is commercially grown blackberries and store bought blackberry jelly, you really don't know what they taste like.

Why is it that I can make myself go to all this trouble for something good to eat, and then throw away something far more valuable because "it's not worth it?" Why does teasing my taste buds matter more to me than saving my soul? How many spiritual delicacies have I missed out on because it wasn't worth the trouble?

Serious Bible study can be tedious, but isn't having the Word of God coming instantly to mind when I really need it worth it? When I have taken the time to explore deeply instead of the superficial knowledge most have, isn't it great in the middle of a sermon or Bible class, to suddenly have another passage spring to life right before my mental eyes? "So that's what that means!" is a eureka moment that is nearly incomparable. And while increased knowledge does not necessarily mean increased faith, faith without knowledge is a sham. "Faith comes by hearing and hearing by the word of God" (Rom 10.17). The more scripture you know, the stronger your faith because the more you know about what God has done for us, the more you appreciate it and want to show that appreciation by the service you willingly give.

So many other things we miss out on because we don't want to go to the trouble—cultivating an active prayer life, socializing with brothers and sisters in the faith, helping a new Christian grow, serving the community we live in simply because we care—while at the same time we go to all sorts of trouble for earthly pleasures—sitting in the hot sun on a hard bench amid crude, rowdy people to watch a ball game; searching for a parking space for hours then walking ten blocks in high heels for a favorite meal at a downtown restaurant; standing in long lines at an amusement park, while someone else's ice cream melts on your shirt, and at the same time juggling your own handfuls of fast food, cameras, and tickets, and trying to keep up with rambunctious children. All these things are "worth it." Did you ever ask yourself, "Worth what?" And how long did that pleasure, or whatever your answer is, last?

I would never go to the same amount of trouble for rhubarb that I do for blackberries. That doesn't mean I don't like rhubarb—I make a pretty good strawberry rhubarb cobbler. But rhubarb cannot match blackberries. Spiritually, we too often settle for rhubarb instead of blackberries. You can always tell the ones who don't "settle"—the "purple" fingers from handling the Word of God, and the "purple" teeth and tongues from taking it in on a daily basis and living a life as His servant, give them away.

> *As for the rich in this present age, charge them not to be haughty, nor to set their hopes on the uncertainty of riches, but on God,* ***who richly provides us with everything to enjoy****. They are to do good, to be rich in good works, to be generous and ready to share, thus storing up treasure for themselves as a good foundation for the future,* ***so that they may take hold of that which is truly life.***
>
> 1 Timothy 6.17–19

42. Sowing the Seed: The Danger of Idealism

A long time ago a young woman I had met in the small town where we lived asked me for some advice. Her marriage was suffering and she didn't know what to do.

I was too young for her to be asking me, but she had found out I was "a preacher's wife," and thought that automatically made me a font of wisdom. When she finally asked her question, my answer came easily (and with a sigh of relief). The problem was a perfect fit for a scripture in Corinthians and I simply had her read what the inspired apostle said about it. I didn't have to say a word.

Her mouth hung open in shock. "That's the answer," she said. "But why haven't my own church leaders been able to show me this verse?" It was not a difficult passage to find. Anyone who has grown up attending Bible classes in the church would know where to find it. The fact that men who called themselves her spiritual leaders could not help her with the same passage gave me an opening, and we began a Bible study that lasted several weeks.

I was far too idealistic. I thought when people saw it in black and white, they would instantly change, and that left me wide open for hurt and discouragement. We finally reached a point where her conscience was pricked and she was floundering about, wondering what to do.

"Would you come again next week and talk to my church

leaders too?" she asked, and what could 22-year-old me say, but "Of course, if you don't mind if my husband comes with me." She agreed enthusiastically.

All of us met the next Tuesday evening at her home, me with all sorts of great expectations, and an hour long discussion ensued. To make a long story short, they simply told us that they had more faith than we did because they would accept a piece of literature as inspired which contained neither internal nor external evidences, the kind of evidences that make the Bible obviously true. I was flabbergasted, and learned my first lesson—some people will believe what they want to believe, not what is reasonable to believe.

The next week I went to her home on Tuesday morning for our usual study. She met me at the door and, with tears in her eyes, she said, "I'm sorry. They told me I can't study with you any more."

"But don't you want to? I helped you when they couldn't."

"I know," she said. "But they are my *leaders*, and I have to obey them."

Talk about discouraging. What do you do when someone who is good-hearted and clearly sees the truth allows herself to be taken in by people who obviously cannot—or will not—even help her with her problems? It isn't just the stubborn and willful who reject the word of God, another new lesson for me to learn. In fact, it takes strength of will to accept it when it means you must stand against friends and family, and when your life will experience an instant upheaval.

So here is the main lesson today: Be careful whom you trust. Be careful whom you allow to direct your path, and have the gumption to take responsibility for your own soul. If someone who wanted the truth could allow it to slip through her fingers so easily at the word of people who were never there for her until it became obvious their numbers might go down, it could happen to you too. The religious leaders in Jesus' day looked down on the people with scorn (John 7.49), yet those very people followed them right down the road to Calvary, berating a man who had stood up for them more than once to those same leaders, pushing him to his crucifixion.

And here is another lesson: don't let your idealism make you vulnerable to discouragement. I will always remember that young woman. We moved far away not long afterward. As far as I know she stayed where she was religiously, and never found her way out of it. But I do have this hope—I planted a seed. God is the one who sees to the increase (1 Cor 3.6). Don't ever in your mind deny God the power to make that seed grow. I am not as idealistic as I used to be, but I still hope that someday I will meet her again, standing among the sheep.

> *But false prophets also arose among the people, just as there will be false teachers among you, who will secretly bring in destructive heresies, even denying the Master who bought them, bringing upon themselves swift destruction. And many will follow their sensuality, and because of them the way of truth will be blasphemed. And in their greed they will exploit you with false words. Their condemnation from long ago is not idle, and their destruction is not asleep.*
>
> 2 Peter 2.1–3

43. Sowing the Seed: Fighting Discouragement

I planted, Apollos watered, but God gave the increase (1 Cor 3.6)

We should probably talk some more about that discouragement issue because it never goes away. You teach and teach and teach; you invite at every opportunity that comes along; you serve and reach out, and yet it seems like nothing comes of it. If you aren't careful, you stop trying. It isn't doing any good, is it? That is *not* for me to say.

I told you before of the young woman I tried to reach so long ago. Just because I have no contact with her now, doesn't mean nothing came of it. I remember having discussions during free periods in high school. I took friends to Bible study with me. I wrote essays in English class that I knew would be passed around the class for comment. I have never seen anything come from any of that, but as Keith often says, I don't need to be whittling on God's end of the stick. *He* is the one who gives the increase. When I start meddling in His affairs, I become disheartened. If I stick with my own end, I will stay too busy to worry about the results.

I suppose my biggest dose of discouragement came a couple of years ago. Some new neighbors had moved in a few years before and she and I became friends. I easily recruited her to a local community service club, but anything religiously oriented was a different story. So I invited her to a coffee at my home where she met some of my church family. So far, so good. I invited her to our women's Bible study, and immediately she distanced herself. Too much too soon, I thought, so I had a church friend whose decorating ability she had shown interest in, invite her to lunch at her home, along with another church sister. An instant yes, but then as the day approached my neighbor suddenly developed something else she had to do.

So I backed off again. I still mentioned the church to her as often as possible, telling her how wonderful they were. I made sure she knew about all the help I received after all the surgeries, and she was genuinely impressed so I invited again, including a written invitation. Still nothing.

Then one day, her husband called to tell me she had died without warning. No one even knew she had been sick. In fact, we had talked on the phone just three days before. It was like a kick in the stomach. I do not believe I have ever felt quite so discouraged in my sowing duties.

That is exactly what the enemy wants, and that is exactly why you need to stop worrying about God's end of the stick. When the depression is accompanied by grief it is especially debilitating. All you need to remember is this: Just. Keep. Sowing!

Since that time I have suddenly had more opportunities to speak to people. God is encouraging me, I thought, so I have tried to do my part as well. I am anything but the Great Evangelist, but here are a few things I have tried.

When I have the car maintenance done, I purposely make the appointment right before ladies' Bible class so I can use the shuttle service to the class. You would be surprised how many drivers want to know what I will be teaching, and then ask about the church. I have even managed to give out a few tracts.

When I buy my groceries I do it before Bible class and then have the bagger put the cold things into my cooler. "I have to teach a Bible class before I go home," I explain, and that has led to conversations too.

I carry my Bible and my notebook to doctor's appointments and write these little essays there. As many appointments as I have, surely someone will be interested some day. Even the cleaning lady recognizes me now.

I have no idea if any of these things will bear fruit, but I do "consider him faithful who has promised," (Heb 11.11), and he promised to see to the growth of the seed if I just sow it.

Don't become depressed when you don't see results from your work. That part is none of your business. Just keep sowing the seed. You do your part, and He will do His.

> *What then is Apollos? What is Paul? Servants through whom you believed, as the Lord assigned to each. I planted, Apollos watered, but God gave the growth. So neither he who plants nor he who waters is anything, but only God who gives the growth. He who plants and he who waters are one, and each will receive his wages according to his labor.*
>
> 1 Corinthians 3.5–8

44. Sowing the Seed: Success

I do not mean to leave you discouraged, so let me share some success stories with you. After all these years, we have a few, and I do believe God meant us to share them with one another (Acts 14.27).

I remember a lot of baptisms. Keith has baptized in swimming pools, sunken bathtubs, and ponds. I remember standing right at the shore, cold water lapping at my feet on a chilly January night as a young woman came up out of the water with him, and wrapping her in blankets as quickly as I could. I remember him coming home one night, sticking his legs out of the truck door to show me the damp hems because a Bible study had resulted in the birth of a babe in Christ. I remember the night we stood on the edge of a swamp, bullfrogs croaking a bass chorus and headlights shining over the weedy waters, as he baptized a young man he had studied with for several weeks. I believe it was May and I remember thinking, surely God will keep the snakes at bay tonight!

I remember some neighbors up the street in another state, who had started coming to services, and her to our women's class, and who wanted so badly to be baptized one Sunday morning, they wouldn't even change into robes. "We came in these clothes, and these clothes are going down with us, right now!" the man said. I think we did persuade him to remove his wallet and take off his shoes.

I remember another young man who faithfully completed the correspondence course, asking good questions along the way, and then sent back his final lesson with the note, "I'm ready to be baptized." He attended faithfully until he moved away. I remember another young man whose commitment was restored after a long talk, who brought his wife to us, and has gone on to begin a church in an area where there was none, still faithful after thirty years

God sends you other encouragements if you just pay attention. One neighbor had seen us leave every Sunday morning, and when suddenly she had custody of her three grandchildren, she called, wanting us to take them to church with us. We certainly would have loved to have her as well, but we didn't look down on the opportunity. For two years those children were dressed and waiting every Sunday morning at 8:00. I have no idea if that has borne fruit, but I do know this—when the woman died, her children asked Keith to speak at her memorial. Something had been planted and it did have some effect. That's all God asked us to do.

Sowing the seed is not a part-time job. For a Christian, it's a career. Get on with it. No one will be judged by the results. Just remember that every person you come across is a potential field and everything you do can affect the results of your planting. That is what you will be judged on, not the number of splashes.

God wants sowers. He wants waterers, and, we hope, plenty of harvesters. The seed *will* yield its crop, but don't get so busy counting ears of corn that you forget to plant the next row.

> *For I am not ashamed of the gospel for it is the power of God unto salvation to everyone who believes, to the Jew first and also to the Gentile.*
>
> Romans 1.16

45. Fungicide

I had a beautiful flower garden last year—brick red gaillardia, their blooms lined with yellow-gold trumpet-shaped petals; pink, magenta, white, and burgundy cosmos fluttering on feathery spring green plumes: hardy, yellow gloriosa daisies shining like beacons among the leaves; yellow, orange, and rust colored marigolds perched on the bushiest plants I had ever seen in that flower; bright purple Mexican petunias who, though they shed their blooms every night, never failed to greet me with another show of dozens every morning; and zinnias sporting every color imaginable—white, yellow, salmon, cherry red, fire engine red, bright orange, purple, pink, lime green, and even variegated colors, growing as tall as five feet before the summer was out.

Unfortunately, those zinnias began growing something besides blooms. It started at the bottom, with black-rimmed white spots on just a few lower leaves. It spread from one plant to several in an area until finally it had touched every single plant. Then it began its inexorable climb until only the top few leaves remained green, and only the newest blossoms, barely opened from the bud, were clean. It took me awhile to realize what was happening, and by the time I figured it out, it was too late.

Still, I didn't want to pull the plants. They did have a little green left at the top, and where there is life there is hope, right? Finally after several mornings of looking out on what had once brought joy to my mornings and seeing instead a mass of black leaves and stems, I made a decision. Why did I have these flowers anyway? Because they were beautiful, and even I could see all that color from a distance. Were they beautiful any longer? No, they were about as ugly as they could be. And the longer I waited, the further that fungus spread. The gaillardia were already infected, and a few of the marigolds.

So the next day I went out and began pulling. It wasn't even laborious. Those plants were so sick that they came right up out of the ground, and do you know what I found underneath? New seedlings growing from the deadheads I had been cutting all summer. If I had left those ugly things much longer, the baby plants would have been choked out by the much larger roots and then infected as well. Now they can breathe and grow, and the sunlight reaches their tiny leaves. I have already gotten out the copper spray, a fungicide that is even considered "organic," not that I would care since my goal is to save those new flowers no matter what it takes, and they aren't on the menu anyway.

Still, it was hard to make that decision. I have trouble even thinning the rows in the vegetable garden. It goes against my nature to pull up a plant that is still alive, even if it does mean better production from the ones you leave, and far more food on my shelves to last the winter.

Sometimes we have to make decisions like that with souls. "Give not that which is holy to the dogs, nor cast your pearls before swine" (Matt 7.6). Who wants to make that judgment call? "And whosoever shall not receive you nor hear your words… shake the dust off your feet (10.14). It is difficult to give up on someone you have invested a lot of time in, someone you have come to care about. But sometimes our refusal to do so is costing many more souls out there the chance to hear and accept the word while we waste time on the stubborn and rebellious.

Sometimes that decision must be made among ourselves too. "A little leaven leavens the whole lump," Paul warned about immorality (1 Cor 5.6), and then used exactly the same warning about false doctrine in Galatians 5.9. If you know anything about cooking, you know that leaven is alive. It may not be a fungus, but it creeps in exactly the same way and spreads. No matter how small a chunk of it you use, that dough will suddenly react, and there is no going back when it does. Speaking of false teachers in 2 Timothy 2.17, Paul says, "Their word eats as does a gangrene." When gangrene eats away the flesh, it's gone.

Yes, we have to make these tough decisions, but I have seen some people make it with a little too much zest. God never enjoyed it. "I have no pleasure in the death of the wicked," He said (Ezek 33.11). God "would have all men to be saved," Paul says (1 Tim 2.4), and Peter reminds us that God "is not willing that any should perish" (2 Pet 3.9). He waited a long time before He finally punished His people, and even then it was with anguish: "How shall I give you up…how shall I cast you off…my heart recoils within me, my compassion grows warm and tender" (Hos 11.8).

God never meant for this decision to be easy, but sometimes it has to be made. It isn't compassion not to make it—it's cowardice. My medical book says that fungus spreads worst among very young children and those who are already ill. We must look underneath those infected branches to see the reason for our decision—to save many more before they too are infected with a fatal disease. The souls who were sacrificed in the arenas by the Roman persecution are depicted as asking God, "How long until you will judge and avenge our blood?" (Rev 6.10). Desperate souls may be out there asking us, How long are you going to waste time on the unwilling, when we want it so badly?"

> *"Rejoice with him, O heavens; bow down to him, all gods, for he avenges the blood of his children and takes vengeance on his adversaries. He repays those who hate him and cleanses his people's land."*
>
> Deuteronomy 32.43

46. Deadheads

We live on five acres, but do not have the equipment to handle it sometimes. Most everything we have accomplished has been with a shovel, a wheelbarrow, and Keith's strong back. We certainly don't have a tractor to keep it manicured properly.

We decided a few years ago that we had rather see some splashes of color here and there instead of waist high green grass and assorted head high weeds, so we planted several cans of mixed wildflower seeds around the perimeter of the mown section. The first year they did not do much, but the second year we had a nice showing of coreopsis, gaillardia, and gloriosa daisies. They come up again every spring and have even spread out into the field in a few places.

Four summers ago I started cutting the deadheads and scattering them around. I thought it might be nice to have some up by the gate to greet our guests and scattered a few up there. The next year I had two orange firewheels, the more colloquial name for gaillardia. The year after that we had about six. Last year I quit counting at 20. They were so thick it was hard to tell exactly how many there were—we're talking plants, not blooms, which were many times more than 20. I can hardly wait to see what happens this year.

You've seen deadheads. They are gray or brown, shriveled and dried up. You would never think they had once been beautiful blooms or were any longer valuable at all. But "deadhead" is a most inaccurate name for them. Inside those ugly old blooms lay the potential for thousands more beautiful blooms.

Have you looked in the mirror lately? Some of you are a lot younger than I, but no matter how young you are, you are not as young as you used to be. Someday you will be my age, and most of you will get even older than that. It's easy these days, especially facing a major disability, to think that I am no longer useful in the kingdom. It's easy to say that since I might not be able to get out much any more, that I cannot serve. When you grow older, you will face the same feelings. If you are older, you may be facing them already.

But that is not the case. Just like those dried up flowers, you have the potential to reach thousands through your example. Maybe the only example you are able to give any more is faithfulness—but it is a powerful one, and always needed. You are there when the doors of the meetinghouse are opened if you can drag yourself out at all. Sometimes you are there when you ought not to be. You have been married for 40, 50, 60 years to the same husband or wife, and the devotion between you is still obvious. You sit quietly and never cause any trouble. In Bible classes you make comments that show you have lived by the scriptures. You have children who are faithful to God, to their mates, to the body of Christ, and who are good citizens of this earthly country as well. Do you think none of that counts?

If you are young, you need to start making good use of these resources. Too many times the young are stuck in the self-centered ways of youth, forgetting that older Christians have lived a life every bit as interesting as theirs. Get them to talking sometime about their past. You just might be amazed at what they have been through and survived; things you will probably never face in these prosperous times. And you will find one of the helps God always intended you to have—the wisdom of the aged. I have learned more valuable lessons from quiet people with halos of silver hair than from any pulpit preacher I have ever listened to—and I have heard some pretty good ones.

Setting an example is not something we have a choice about. As long as we are alive we do just that. And it may be the most powerful thing any of us do. You are never shriveled, dried up and useless as far as God is concerned. You are always sowing seeds. Be sure you sow the right ones.

> *The hoary head is a crown of glory; it shall be found in the way of righteousness.*
>
> Proverbs 16.31

47. Weeding with a Vengeance

I had heard bad news the night before, and after a night of crying and praying, had completely passed the grief stage and was well into rage. I furiously weeded the flower beds, flinging dirt and weeds as hard as I could. At least it served a purpose. In Florida, you can't just hoe the weeds and expect them to die. Anything green will re-root by morning in this humid climate unless you completely remove it from the garden.

I was black to my elbows and sweating profusely when it crossed my mind to wonder if it might just be all right to curse if I were cursing Satan. Chloe sat next to me, tilting her head back and forth in confusion. Finally, when the convulsive sobbing started, she tucked her tail between her legs and slunk off in the direction of the porch, with a bewildered look over her shoulder at me.

In a moment of clarity awhile later, I realized that I had reached a milestone in my spiritual life. Automatically, without even having to think about it, I had directed my rage at the right person. Instead of blaming God, I had blamed the one who twists every good thing into ugliness. For once I had never even had a question about why this thing had happened. I knew why it had happened—because the enemy of God is the enemy of every one of his faithful children too.

So why doesn't God keep anything bad from happening to those children? Maybe the same reason a good parent doesn't shield his child from the result of his own mistakes. Maybe the same reason we make them eat their vegetables and get their shots. Causing pain is not always bad, not if you want to build healthy bodies and strong characters. But who am I to even ask or say anything definitive about the matter? This is all I can say:

> His faithfulness is everlasting. (Psa 119.90)
>
> He loves justice and will not forsake his saints. (Psa 37.28)
>
> His love is steadfast (Psa 89.2)
>
> There is no unrighteousness in him. (Psa 92.15)
>
> He made all things very good (Gen 1.31), and is the only one who is good. (Luke 18.19)
>
> He cannot be tempted with evil, and is never the cause of temptation. (Jas 1.13)

Does any of that sound like the one we should blame about anything? Most of our problems come because of the freewill God created in us, yet even that freewill is a good thing for it means we can *choose* to love and serve God rather than being the pawns of a pagan notion of destiny. It means He can know that our service is willing and not forced, and that our love for Him is just as genuine as His for us.

That means we will have to put up with things we don't like, with things that hurt and cause us pain because a long time ago one of us chose the wrong way, and suddenly there was evil in the world. But isn't it wonderful that the justice of God says that, while we may have to live with the effects of that choice, we aren't saddled with its guilt—we can make our own choices.

Remember when bad things befall you who to blame. Go out to your flower beds and remind yourself what the scriptures call him each time you rip out a weed and fling it with all your might—the Accuser, the Adversary, the Enemy, the Evil One, the father of lies, the Prince of demons, the Ruler of this world, that old Serpent, the Tempter. Why in the world would we ever think Someone Else was to blame?

This I recall to my mind; therefore have I hope. It is of Jehovah's lovingkindnesses that we are not consumed, because his compassions fail not. They are new every morning; great is thy faithfulness. Jehovah is my portion, saith my soul; therefore will I hope in him. Jehovah is good unto them that wait for him, to the soul that seeks him. It is good that a man should hope and quietly wait for the salvation of Jehovah.

Lamentations 3.21–26

48. The Return of the Parsley Worms

All summer I had been watching those monarch butterflies flit over my flower beds. Every couple of days I carefully checked the herb garden twenty feet away for signs of their caterpillars. That's what I read somewhere—that monarch butterfly caterpillars are the dreaded parsley worms that can wreak havoc on that herb almost overnight. Nothing happened. My parsley grew well and was never infested. Somehow I got off easy this year. I thought.

Then in mid-October we went away for a week. We returned on a Friday night, after dark, too late to see much but the back porch by the light hanging outside the back door. The next morning we stepped out for a stroll and saw what had happened. Every sprig of parsley was completely bare, only the bright green stems sticking up completely naked—except here and there for the bright green worm still clinging to the bush it had just decimated. I am not so paranoid as to think that somehow they all got together and planned the attack for while we were away, but it was certainly suspicious.

Satan, on the other hand, is perfectly capable of planning his attacks that way. He waits until we are most vulnerable. He waits until we have experienced a crisis in our lives, until we are frustrated by circumstances, until our defenses are down, and then he zooms in for the kill. Being on the alert when you are tired and hurt is not easy, but that is exactly what we must do, standing guard as a soldier in the Lord's army.

One of the greatest benefits of being in the family of God is having people who care enough to watch your back. All of us should be aware of the crises in our brothers and sisters' lives. Too often we are so consumed with our own affairs that we don't have time to watch out for others, and that means we are *too* consumed, period. Then we wonder how a brother could fall so far, why a sister was caught up in such a sin, why a family has "suddenly" disappeared from among us. How in the world could those things have happened? They happened in part because everyone was too busy to notice.

What do you do when announcements are made in the assembly? Is that when you spend your time arranging your books, glasses, and children on the pew, the time you flip to the first song and look through it, the time you know you can spend a little longer in the ladies' room before you need to be seated? Those announcements should be your greatest tool the next week as you figure out what you need to do for whom, how you can encourage a brother or sister in distress, what you might say to one whose soul is in danger. How much do you hear when you are finishing up a conversation that has no bearing on a soul, or racing to your pew before the first song begins? Those pieces of news are about service, and that is the most important part of a Christian's life, "considering one another" (Heb 10.24).

Be aware of the timing in the lives of others too. Is it the first anniversary of a widow's loss? Is it a season that makes being alone that much harder for the single? Are ordeals approaching in people's lives that might make them more prone to Satan's attacks? We have a job to do; we have service to offer; we have comfort to give and sometimes exhortation and rebuke when we see those attacks making progress in the lives of another.

If we see them. If we care. If we aren't so wrapped up in ourselves that we miss the attacks and wake up one morning to an almost overnight slaughter in the garden of God.

Wherefore lift up the hands that hang down, and the palsied knees; and make straight paths for your feet, that that which is lame be not turned out of the way, but rather be healed.

Hebrews 12.12–13

49. A Long Hard Winter

In Florida "winter" means very little, but a year or so ago we had a different sort of winter—long cold spells with lows below freezing and highs only in the 40s, and frosts as late as April. Snow fell in the panhandle and in the north central peninsula. Usually we are sorry to see the heat return, but that year we were longing for it.

The spring was different too. The azaleas bloomed two months later, and all at the same time, so profusely you couldn't even see the branches. The blueberries had more fruit on them than any time in the five years past. The hostas not only came up again but multiplied, sending up four plants where each one plant sat the year before. The spring wildflowers were beautiful, turning fields first into blankets of blue and lavender, then red and maroon, and finally pink and white. The oak pollen fell so thickly the lawn looked like wall to wall brown carpeting. And the garden produced better than it had in years.

I wondered, could one thing have to do with the other? Could a long, hard winter be the cause of good crops and beautiful flowers in the spring?

"And they arrested [Peter and John] and put them in custody until the next day because it was already evening. But many of those who heard the word believed and the number of men came to about five thousand" (Acts 4.3–4). That is not the only case in the New Testament where rapid growth of the kingdom followed hard on the heels of persecution. A long hard winter of trial always seemed to make for a springtime of growth among God's people.

Then there is the personal aspect. I have seen so many times how a personal trial has led to spiritual growth in a Christian. I have experienced it myself. Something about trial inures us to the pains that might otherwise cost us our souls. We grow stronger little by little, gradually learning the lessons of faith, endurance and strength in the service of God.

That may be why I cringe when I see a young mother turn every little scrape on the knee or cut on the finger into a life-threatening crisis worthy of the loudest wails, instead of helping her child learn to laugh it off. I have seen too many of those children grow into men and women who complain about everything that does not go their way. If it's okay to whine and cry like the world is ending when you fall and skin your knees, why isn't it okay to scream at other drivers who get in your way? If it's okay to pout and mope when you don't get to play your favorite video game, why isn't it okay to complain long and loud when the boss asks you to work overtime? If it's okay to pitch a fit when some mean adult tells you to straighten up, why isn't it okay to stand in the parking lot complaining about the church, the preachers, the elders, and anyone else who doesn't see things your way?

God needs people who are strong, who can take pain and suffering for His sake, who understand that their way doesn't really matter if it is not His way, and that the good of the kingdom and its mission may have nothing to do with them having an easy, perfect life here in this world, but everything to do with a perfect life in the next.

Just as with everything else, our culture is affecting us. The strong silent type who can take the worst the world has to offer and keep going is no longer the hero. Instead we reward jerks and boors and idolize intemperance. Prodigality and lavish lifestyles are our measure of success; striking back is our measure of character, and throwing tantrums is our measure of strength.

I see a day coming when the church will once again be in the middle of a long, hard winter of persecution. The way we are going we may not survive it at all, let alone have a bountiful spring, because trials and persecution only work to build strength when you learn from them. They only produce character when you have the toughness to take the bad with the good without whining about it.

What kind of spring will you have next year?

> *And not only so but we rejoice in our tribulations, knowing that tribulation works steadfastness; and steadfastness approvedness; and approvedness hope; and hope puts not to shame, because the love of God has been shed abroad in our hearts through the Holy Spirit which was given unto us.*
>
> Romans 5.3–5

50. Pluots

We first discovered pluots three or four years ago when we set about to try one new fruit or vegetable a week. We have discovered many yummy treats, most too expensive to enjoy regularly or in any volume, but pluots, a cross between plums and apricots, are reasonably priced in season, and delicious.

Hybrids can be a good thing, increasing size and yield, and creating resistance to certain plant diseases. Hybrids can also be a bad thing, dulling flavor distinctions and, of course, making it impossible to save the seeds for next year, thus increasing the cost of gardening. Heirloom varieties are becoming popular for a reason.

Sometimes when we sow the seed, instead of creating "heirloom Christians," we wind up with hybrids. The best way to avoid that is to make sure we are good old fashioned New Testament Christians ourselves, with no trace of sectarianism in us.

Do any of the mainstream "isms" show up in your language and thinking?

"Lord, we know we sin all the time." Sounds like total depravity to me.

"I know I'm not living right, but at least I've been baptized." Am I hearing once saved always saved?

"The preacher didn't visit me in the hospital." You did say "preacher" didn't you? Or do you mean "pastor?"

Allowing denominational practices to warp our understanding of the simple gospel can lead to all sorts of problems, not the least of which is a congregation that becomes far more like its denominational neighbors than like its first century sisters. When we expect a preacher to spend more time holding hands than holding Bible studies, when our traditions and our language show signs of various manmade doctrines instead of the simple elements found in the epistles, we need to check our bloodlines.

I pointed out how a certain activity was performed in the New Testament once, only to have someone say in a startled tone, "That would never fly here." If it's simply a matter of expedience, fine. After all, it is 2,000 years removed. But if it's because we've allowed faulty understanding from a past of bad theology to taint our thinking, it's not.

God doesn't want hybrid Christians, not even pluots. He wants a people who approach His word and His divine institution with pure hearts and minds, unadulterated from years of false teaching. In God's eyes, there are no good hybrids, just defiled pedigrees.

> *Moreover all the chiefs of the priests, and the people, trespassed very greatly after all the abominations of the nations; and they polluted the house of Jehovah which he had hallowed in Jerusalem.*
>
> 2 Chronicles 36.14

> *That he might present the church to himself a glorious church, not having spot or wrinkle or any such thing; but that it should be holy and without blemish.*
>
> Ephesians 5.27

51. What I Did on My Summer Vacation

The garden has come and gone in the past six weeks. Day after hot, humid day I stood in the kitchen, scalding, blanching, peeling, seeding, chopping, mixing, packing, freezing, pickling, preserving and canning. After an hour or more in the garden, followed by six hours of standing in the kitchen, my back ached, my feet throbbed, and I had a knot between my shoulders blades. Then the next day I got up and did it again. In the evenings we shelled and snapped until midnight or our hands ached too much to continue, whichever came first.

So why did I do it? Because it had to be done. This is one way we manage not only to survive on what we make, but to eat fairly well in spite of what we make. This is how we fed two teenage boys and remained financially solvent. And it wasn't all bad.

Some days I managed to do a lot of meditating while I worked. When you must do the same action over and over, like peeling four hundred tomatoes, it becomes automatic, so you can use your mind for better things, pondering recent lessons you have heard, drawing conclusions from verses you have read, and praying through some of the problems that beset you.

Keith took a few days off during all this to help me out. I am not quite what I used to be, and the live-in help left quite a few years ago. We cannot "chat" over our work as most couples can. Sometimes I touched his arm to get his attention so I could tell him something I thought important. Other times he spoke (since I don't have to see to hear) and then I could reply when he looked up. Once or twice we got into a friendly competition. He still cannot fill a jar as quickly as I can—his hands are bigger and not as well trained, but what he could do still meant jars I did not have to fill myself. And even after thirty-nine years, or more probably because of them, it was pleasant to be together.

The other day Lucas said something like, "Isn't it funny how we look forward to the garden starting, and then near the end look forward to it ending?" And he is right—except for the chili peppers and the grapes, things are nearly at an end, and I am glad. Still, at the end of each day's work the past month, I looked on the rows of jars cooling on an old rag of a towel laid across the countertop and felt a sense of accomplishment, despite the occasional tedium, the many aches, and the pools of sweat on the floor from the rising steam in the kitchen.

I wish you could see my pantry—23 jars of tomatoes, 15 jars of salsa, 18 jars of dill pickles, a dozen jars each of okra dills and pickled banana pepper rings, and 30 jars of three kinds of jellies and jams. Then open the freezer—two dozen bags of corn, 20 bags of green beans, ten bags of lima beans, eight bags of zipper cream peas, 12 quarts of tomato sauce, and eight quarts of blueberries. The best is yet to come though, when my grocery bill totals half what it might have been and ultimately, when we eat it all.

So maybe it was not what some might consider a "summer vacation." In fact, I also had a couple of days worth of testing at the eye clinic mixed in there somewhere, but it was a worthwhile venture that did us far more good than tanning at a beach might have.

I think living a Christian life might be the same sort of vacation. Some days it is hard work. Some days it is tedious. Some days it causes us pain. But we can make even the worst days better by meditating on the comfort in God's word, and by talking to Him whenever we want to. We have a spiritual family who will help bear our burdens, who will weep when we weep and rejoice when we rejoice, people who will make the bad days go quicker and the good days even happier.

And then before you know it, it's almost over. But there are things we can look back on with satisfaction, unlike our friends in the world who will have so much to regret. They will also have nothing to look forward to, while for us the best is yet to come, and aren't we looking forward to that?

For all of us summer will soon turn to fall, and after that the winter. Make sure your pantry is full.

> *And I heard the voice from heaven saying, Write, Blessed are the dead who die in the Lord from henceforth, yes, says the Spirit, that they may rest from their labors, for their works follow with them.*
>
> Revelation 14.13

52. Walking in the Garden

Yes, God must have loved gardens. That first garden was used as the ideal all through the scriptures, the utopia that everyone longed for. The Messianic kingdom is referred to as the restoration of the Garden of Eden in Isaiah, Jeremiah, Ezekiel and other prophets.

> "And the land that was desolate shall be tilled, instead of being the desolation that it was in the sight of all who passed by. And they will say, 'This land that was desolate has become like the garden of Eden, and the waste and desolate and ruined cities are now fortified and inhabited.' Then the nations that are left all around you shall know that I am the LORD; I have rebuilt the ruined places and replanted that which was desolate. I am the LORD; I have spoken, and I will do it." (Ezek 36.34–36)

And why was Eden perfect? Everything man needed was in that first garden, trees and plants to sustain his physical life, including the Tree of Life. God also gave man the companionship of a woman, for He said, "it is not good that man should be alone" (Gen 2.18). He gave him work to do, tending that garden, and every evening He came to walk with man. Surely that marvelous fellowship was the greatest need He fulfilled.

Revelation 22 depicts another garden, one that despite my growing belief that the majority of the descriptions in that book are about the victorious church, I cannot help but see in a final heavenly fulfillment. We will be back where the Tree of

Life spreads its branches (22.2). We will be with other servants of God, "those whose names are written in the Lamb's book of life" (21.27). We will have work—to serve and worship our Creator for Eternity (22.3, 8–9). And once again we will be in fellowship, and proximity, to God—His throne is there and we shall "see his face" (22.1, 4). God's plan will have come full circle, from that first garden to an eternal one.

But there was another garden, one right in the middle of it all—Gethsemane. It had some of the same characteristics. The disciples had fellowship with each other and with their Lord. And they had work to do. "Watch with me," Jesus told them (Matt 26.38). It had been a long day, one full of surprises and mysterious statements by their Master. They were tired, wanting only to rest, and so "their eyes were heavy," and they slept (26.43). When the Lord needed them most, they failed Him.

That garden was the reason we have hope of an Eternal Garden. In a sense, we are living our lives in that middle garden with the Lord. "Watch and pray that you enter not into temptation," he told those men (Mark 14.38), adding at the end, "the spirit is willing, but the flesh is weak." My flesh may indeed be weak, but too often my spirit is lacking as well. Life can wear you out. Trials seem to come in one long succession, like a string of ugly beads. All you want to do is have one day of peace, one day when something goes right, when it seems like the world isn't against you and justice will prevail.

It *is* hard, and your Lord knows it. He sat in that same garden you are in now, awaiting things you will probably never have to experience. And he did it so you can have hope of a garden where everything will finally be right, where you can rest and "there will be no curse any more."

But for now, you must watch, you must endure just a little while longer. I have finally lived long enough to know that it isn't that long a "while" till it's over, and then "there shall be night no more; and they need no light of lamp, neither light of sun; for the Lord God shall give them light: and they shall reign for ever and ever."

And once again, we will walk in the garden with God.

> *He that has an ear, let him hear what the Spirit says to the churches. To him that overcomes, to him will I give to eat of the tree of life, which is in the Paradise of God.*
>
> Revelation 2.7

Also by Dene Ward

Soul Food

Lessons from Hearth to Heart

Cooking has always been a part of Dene Ward's life. She grew up in a house where they were always feeding someone and followed that same path as a wife and mother. On the table, she has always offered a nourishing meal; she now offers this collection to feed your souls, lessons from her hearth to your heart.148 pages. $9.99 (PB)

Flight Paths

A Devotional Guide for your Journey

When encroaching blindness took her music teaching career away, Dene Ward turned her attention to writing. What began as e-mail devotions to some friends grew into a list of hundreds of subscribers. Three hundred sixty-six of those devotions have been assembled to form this daily devotional. Follow her through a year of camping, bird-watching, medical procedures, piano lessons, memories, and more as she uses daily life as a springboard to thought-provoking and character-challenging messages of endurance and faith. 475 pages. $18.99 (PB)

More from DeWard

By Paul Earnhart

Invitation to a Spiritual Revolution

Studies in the Sermon on the Mount

Few preachers have studied the Sermon on the Mount as intensively or spoken on its contents so frequently and effectively as the author of this work. His excellent and very readable written analysis appeared first as a series of articles in *Christianity Magazine.* By popular demand it is here offered in one volume so that it can be more easily preserved, circulated, read, reread and made available to those who would not otherwise have access to it. Foreword by Sewell Hall. 173 pages. $9.99 (PB)

Glimpses of Eternity

Studies in the Parables of Jesus

The parables of Jesus are the compelling stories and illustrations from our familiar world which the Lord used to open windows for us into heaven. They help us to understand the heart of God and the nature of the spiritual kingdom which His Son has brought into the world at such an awful cost. There are messages of comfort in the parables and some stern warnings too. They are best understood by those who have a longing to know God's Son and to follow Him in genuine earnestness. These studies are the compilation of a series of articles written for *Christianity Magazine.* 198 pages. $11.99 (PB)

Two Men: Articles on Practical Christian Living
Bill Hall

Brief articles contrasting different characters fill about one-fourth of the book, thus the title, *Two Men*. The men described remind us of people we know, and sometime of ourselves, as we see qualities both good and bad so graphically described. Such portraits should encourage self-improvement. The remaining articles are equally practical, dealing with such subjects as family, church, doctrinal questions and Christian living, providing godly wisdom for dealing with real life situations. 180 pages. $11.99 (PB)

A Worthy Woman (revised edition)
Darlene Craig

Proverbs 31 presents a strong, joyful woman of wisdom, integrity, devotion, talent, industry, compassion, faith and influence. Darlene uses the example of the ideal woman to strengthen and encourage real women of all ages to further realize their "far above rubies" value as they joyfully strive to positively impact the lives of their families and others. 194 pages. $11.99 (PB)

For a full listing of DeWard Publishing Company books, visit our website:

www.deward.com

CPSIA information can be obtained at www.ICGtesting.com
Printed in the USA
BVOW04s0450251114

376578BV00001B/1/P